High Performance Rowing

HIGH PERFORMANCE
ROWING

John McArthur

The Crowood Press

First published in 1997 by
The Crowood Press Ltd
Ramsbury, Marlborough
Wiltshire SN8 2HR

www.crowood.com

This impression 2005

**British Library Cataloguing in Publication
Data**

A catalogue record for this book is available
from the British Library.

ISBN 1 86126 039 3

Throughout this book 'he', 'him' and 'his'
have been used as neutral pronouns and as
such refer to both males and females.

Typeset by Phoenix Typesetting, Ilkley, West
Yorkshire.

Printed and bound in Great Britain by
CPI Bath

Contents

Dedication and Acknowledgements

DEDICATION

This book is dedicated to my Nana and Papa for their endless love and support.

ACKNOWLEDGEMENTS

I would like to express my sincere thanks to everyone who helped me get started, offered their support in times of need and pushed me to complete this book. In particular I would like to thank my reviewers, Nigel, Pete, Simon, Mike, Richard and Mark for their constructive comments on the content and eventual shape of the text. Thanks are also due to my models, Matthew, Kingsley, Tim, Dave and Alaister, for their patience. For taking the time to read the full script and write a Foreword, I extend my most humble thanks to Peter.

I would also like to acknowledge the support of the Amateur Rowing Association and the *Fédération Internationale des Sociétés D'Aviron* in allowing me to use material from their respective coach education programmes and to John Shore for the photographs on the front and back covers. Finally, a special thank you to Laew for putting up with everything and supporting me throughout my many ventures.

Foreword

This book should be required reading for everyone involved in rowing, whether they are a rower or a coach. It is user-friendly and written in an engaging and informative style, making it extremely easy to read.

John's obvious knowledge and enthusiasm for the sport comes through clearly from the very first sentence to the last. He manages to demystify many of the 'secrets' of rowing, taking the reader step by step through the basic fundamentals of technique and training, enabling the information to be absorbed with ease.

The building blocks which I believe are fundamental to moving a boat quickly are explored and explained in a refreshing way. John manages to strip away the jargon, clearly separating the essential facts from the surrounding complications. In doing so he has somehow managed to impart technical knowledge which is applicable whether you are a bridesmaid or a master of your sport.

Unlike many authors who only *present* the information, John helps readers appreciate and understand the multi-faceted approach necessary for top class performance. With this understanding comes the ability to use the information to improve your own rowing or coaching.

The chapter on technical exercises is particularly useful for helping both rower and coach appreciate the need for absolute attention to detail and for the need to share the same goals, technical or otherwise. The detailed coaching points in themselves are worth their weight in gold. As someone who has spent many long hours in a single sculling boat trying to stay fully focused, I found his advice invaluable.

Over the years I have spent many hours discussing with colleagues the best way to move a rowing boat quickly. One of the keys seems to be the need for the rower to be in complete harmony with the boat and the water. This is easier said than done, however, and can prove very elusive. In his determination to make rowing as easy as possible, John has experimented with many different ways of helping rowers achieve this harmony and somehow manages to convey something of this in his writing. I feel certain that anyone who has been coached by him will recognize many of the sentiments expressed here.

I could almost write a book myself in highlighting the other areas that I feel are of particular benefit to readers. I will restrict myself to mentioning the chapters on training and training programmes.

Perhaps for the first time a successful coach has managed to present all the factors needed for success at the highest levels in a clear and easy to understand way. As with the rest of the book he keeps everything as simple as possible whilst passing on the relevant facts.

Like many rowers I have, in the past, relied on my coach to prepare a suitable training programme for me, thereby allowing me to concentrate my efforts on rowing.

If you want to have control over your own destiny, however, you need to understand and influence anything and everything that will have a bearing on it; this includes the training you do. The guidance that John provides will enable you to write your own training programme, giving you more influence over your own destiny. At the very least it will give you a better understanding of what training you should do, when you should do it and how much you should aim to do.

I have known John for many years and respect both his quest for excellence in coaching others and his persistence in pursuing his own goals. I hope you enjoy reading this book as much as I did; I wanted it to last longer and relish the opportunity to review his next book on the subject.

Peter Moir Haining MBE
World Champion, Lightweight Single Sculls 1993, 1994, 1995

Introduction

When I was first approached to write about rowing, I wasn't sure whether I wanted to take on the task of writing an entire book; although I was flattered to be asked, I did not relish the thought of spending many hours in front of a computer screen. However, now that it is complete I realize how good was the opportunity I had been presented with. To be able to share my experiences and thoughts on rowing with others has been very rewarding – indeed, the reason I became involved in coaching in the first place was to do just that: to help others achieve their aims.

Having agreed to write the book, I had to establish what I wanted it to achieve. I decided early on that it needed to be aimed not just at beginners, but also at more experienced rowers and coaches, people who wanted something more than an overall guide to rowing. I have therefore tried to answer some of the many questions I am asked on a regular basis. For example I am often asked to write a training programme, or to advise on the sort of training that should be done at certain times of the year. Similarly coaches often ask what exercises they might use to help their crews with particular technical challenges.

My main aims have therefore been to enable any rower or coach to construct some form of training programme, to know what types of training are appropriate, and to provide guidance as to how to maximize the effect of their training. I have also tried to give some fresh ideas on how to improve technique. Although the book has been written from a coach's perspective, any athlete who seriously wants to go faster will benefit from reading it in its entirety, rather than just the 'interesting' bits. I would particularly encourage readers to study the section on effective coaching (Chapter 6), as many of the points made will help improve rowing technique.

From a coaching point of view I have attempted to dispel some of the myths surrounding rowing. One example that springs to mind is the conviction that the hands need to be very fast away at the finish of the stroke: this is simply not true. You may not agree with some of my arguments, but I hope that you will at least go away and experiment with them.

If you agree with the points I make I shall be happy. If, on the other hand, the book challenges some of your existing ideas, I will be happier still. And if it forces you to look at your beliefs and try new ideas, then I will have achieved one of my main aims: to promote experimentation, for without experimenting we can never progress. Remember: 'If you keep doing what you are doing, you will keep getting what you have got.'

1 Rowing Technique

One of the most common misconceptions as regards rowing is that there are many different techniques to choose from. Coaches often seem to think that in order to be successful they need to know the secret of a particular rowing technique, but this is not the case. Most successful rowing nations are in general agreement as to what is efficient, namely that a quick lively connection is required at the moment the blade enters the water, that the blade should be accelerated throughout the stroke, and that the movement of the recovery should be as relaxed and controlled as possible.

Where differences do occur is in the particular emphasis that each coach places on the elements that make up good technique. For example, some consider it very important to develop a fast accelerated finish, whereas others will concentrate more on the application of power at the catch. What must be remembered is that there is no such thing as a rower with perfect technique, and I have yet to meet a coach (or an international rower) who was 100 per cent satisfied with the technique of his crew. What we see therefore when we look at a crew is the state of its technique *at that moment in time*, and this is not necessarily the end product.

Many might believe that the technique of those top class rowers who have been coached by the same coach for many years must have reached the stage where it represented exactly what they and their coach had been striving to attain. This cannot be the case however, because if ever it was considered that technique had reached perfection, there would be

no room for improvement and complacency would set in. Besides, as the biomechanics and physiology of rowing are better understood, so technique has gradually improved. Thus it is rare these days to find the extremes of body movements seen in the past, and on the whole, the movement of the body – and in particular its upward movement – during the rowing stroke has become more subdued and subtle. The emphasis is on minimizing any upward movement, whilst putting the body in a mechanically advantageous position throughout the stroke. In addition it is important to guard against any excess expenditure of energy in the recovery part of the stroke.

ACHIEVING MAXIMUM BOAT SPEED

Good rowing technique is composed of two different phases: the propulsive phase, when the blades are in the water, and the recovery phase when they are out of the water. It has been argued that since the boat continues to accelerate during the initial part of the recovery, this part of the stroke should also be classified as part of the propulsive phase. However, as a rower is constantly trying to minimize the effects of acceleration and deceleration, I feel that the above classification of the phases is more appropriate.

In order to achieve maximum boat speed you need to maximize the horizontal application of power during the propulsive phase of the stroke, and to minimize the effect of the movement of the crew towards the stern during the recovery phase. To achieve this, it is essential that you have an understanding of the effect that you have on the boat speed. Thus, there is very little point in trying to increase the boat speed by applying more power at the catch if at the same time you are rushing up the slide during the recovery, because the one movement would cancel out the effect of the other. You need therefore to understand from the outset the idea of *economy of movement.*

At its most simple this means accepting that for everything you do in the boat you pay a price in the form of a certain energy requirement: so if you accept that you have only a certain amount of energy available, then you must ensure that where possible, everything you do contributes to the boat speed. In an ideal world, those movements that do not directly contribute to boat speed would be eliminated altogether, although in rowing, as in other sports, this is not possible. You need therefore to ensure that these movements use as little energy as possible, particularly during the recovery phase when the movement towards the stern should be controlled and unhurried.

In practice this means avoiding all unnecessary movements of the head and shoulders and the arms and hands; and perhaps more importantly, you need to ensure that when the correct body position has been reached, it is maintained until the blade is fully covered. It should be clear from this statement that the body plays no part in covering the blade at the catch, which should be initiated by lifting the arms, and not by lifting the body and shoulders. The sequence of movements at the catch is to raise the hands to cover the blade fully, whilst at the same time quickly pushing the legs down. You must never lose sight of the fact that the instant the blade enters the water it acts as a brake, slowing the boat down; thus in order to maximize boat speed it is necessary to minimize this braking effect.

This movement is perhaps the most difficult part of good rowing technique, involving as it does a rapid change of direction. The back and abdominal muscles should remain braced so as to absorb the energy created by the leg drive. Failure to brace these muscles will result in a rapid shooting of the legs towards the bow of the boat, without any commensurate forward movement of the boat. This is commonly known as 'shooting the slide' or 'bum-shoving', and young rowers are often guilty of this habit. This may in fact be due to insufficient development of their back and abdominal muscles; they have often developed relatively strong leg muscles, but have paid insufficient attention to those of their back and abdomen. Having said this, it can also be caused by insufficient attention to technique during the initial stages of learning; too often good technique is sacrificed in order to get the crew racing as soon as possible.

In my opinion, far too many junior and novice rowers are introduced to racing before their technical ability matches their enthusiasm (or their coach's enthusiasm) for racing. This lack of attention to basic rowing technique in the initial stages makes it far more difficult to teach rowers good technique in later years, so that coaching often becomes a matter of eradicating long-standing flaws in technique, rather than helping the rower genuinely to progress in technical ability.

·TECHNIQUE FROM START TO FINISH

In the following detailed description of modern rowing technique I have emphasized those coaching points that I consider to be of most significance. I have divided the stroke into four distinct phases: the entry of the blade, the propulsive phase, the extraction of

11

the blade and the recovery phase – although I hasten to point out that this division is merely to enable a proper explanation of the various components which make up an individual rowing stroke. It goes without saying that when actually rowing, the objective should be a smooth continuous movement from one part of the stroke to the next, and from one stroke to another, and **there should be no discernible start or stop point throughout the entire cycle**. If you can identify any such hiatus then you should examine your technique carefully and should work on keeping everything flowing.

The Entry of the Blade

Your body should be in a strong, tall position with relatively little forward pivot of the upper body. It is essential at this stage that your head is held up and that you are looking towards and beyond the stern of the boat. Your shins should be vertical, with your knees at a natural width apart, that is, not closed together and not wide apart.

Your outside shoulder should be rotated towards the rigger, following the line of the oar handle, and it should be slightly higher than your inside shoulder. Your arms should be in an extended position, with the hands approximately two hand-widths apart. Your wrists should be horizontal (flat), with the fingers hooked around the handle. **The entry of the blade should be initiated using a rapid lifting of your hands and arms whilst keeping your shoulders parallel to the boat.**

The Propulsive Phase

The propulsive phase should be initiated by a strong, forceful acceleration of the leg muscles. At this stage **the back and abdominal muscles should be braced** in order to provide a strong link between the blade and the legs; failure to maintain this bracing of the back will result in the rower shooting the slide, with a subsequent lack of efficient boat propulsion. At the same time as pushing the legs down, **the shoulders should start to accelerate towards the bow of the boat.**

The catch position.

Rotation of the outside shoulder

The propulsive phase.

As the shoulders start to reach the finish of the stroke, the arms should draw powerfully to the body in order to maintain the boat's acceleration past the blade. **Particular emphasis should be placed on the outside arm and shoulder, as these provide the maximum leverage on the blade.**

At the finish of the stroke the body should be in a relaxed but upright position. The shoulders should be just past the vertical point and should be at the same height, relative to the boat, as they were at the catch, whilst the outside arm should draw in close to the body – it should not stick out to the side.

The Extraction of the Blade

The extraction of the blade is performed by tapping down with the outside hand *just before the body* until the blade has cleared the water. **At no point should the oar handle touch the body because this will cause a** **break in the flow of the stroke.** The outside hand should then push the handle away, whilst the inside hand turns the blade to the feathered position. It is essential that the blade is clear of the water before it is feathered. If it is not, a messy finish will result, and this may upset the balance of the boat and will almost certainly slow it down.

The hands should move away at the same speed as they came in to the body. Contrary to popular opinion, there is absolutely no reason for pushing the hands away very fast. Even at high boat speeds, the speed of the hands should mirror that of the boat, and anything faster will work actively against the run of the boat.

The Recovery Phase

The time-honoured sequence for the recovery movement of hands, body, slide, still holds true today. The aim should be to extend the

The finish position.

The body position as you come on to the slides.

arms until they are straight, to **pivot from the hips until the body is in the correct position for the catch**, and only then to start breaking the knees to slide forwards.

It is imperative that the hands are past the knees before starting to move forwards on the slide. Many coaches teach that the body should have reached the catch position by the halfway stage of sliding forwards. Although I can see the merit in this, I prefer the rower to reach this position *before he starts to move the slide*. This allows for greater precision, as it is far easier for him to identify the point at which the slide starts to move forwards, than to judge when it reaches the halfway stage. As with most aspects of rowing technique, **what matters most is that everyone does the same thing at the same time**.

As the body pivots across, the weight will be transferred to the toes. This is one of the most important parts of the entire rowing movement and, in a crew boat in particular, failure to transfer the weight at the same time will disrupt the run of the boat, causing it to slow down. For the same reason – and this is another key point for crew boats – **everyone should begin to move forwards on the slide at the same time**. Although this may seem obvious, in practice it does not always happen.

The speed of the movement towards frontstops should be controlled, and again should be relative to the speed of the boat. It is essential that as you approach frontstops, you prepare yourself to change direction quickly: if you rush in to frontstops it will not be possible for you to do this, and inevitably you will slow the boat down. This means that **from the moment the blade comes out of the water, you should be preparing yourself to change direction at the catch**.

Rowing technique – the complete sequence.

The 1996 world silver medallists lightweight men's eight (Denmark).

The 1996 Great Britain lightweight men's eight, demonstrating the similarities in technique between top crews.

2 Sculling Technique

Sculling is slightly more complicated than rowing as two oars are used instead of one, and the constant adjustment of the hands to allow the oar handles to cross over without touching is particularly difficult for many rowers. Opinions vary as to the most effective way of achieving this. Some coaches advocate that one oar handle is carried higher than the other, whilst others feel that one hand should be in front of the other. The technique currently advocated in Great Britain is that the hands should remain level throughout the stroke, with the left hand leading during the recovery phase. This situation is reversed during the propulsive phase, where the right hand should lead the left towards the body. It is this technique that we shall look at.

There is also considerable discussion as to whether the swivels should be set at the same height, or adjusted so that the bow-side swivel is slightly higher. In line with the technique discussed, and for the purpose of this chapter, the bow-side swivel may be set slightly higher than the stroke side. (For more information on rigging, see Chapter 4.)

It should be understood that all my comments in relation to rowing technique regarding economy of movement and so on, apply equally to sculling. I have also once again divided the stroke into four parts, in the same way as before.

The Entry of the Blade

The body should be in a strong, tall, upright position, with less forward body angle than in rowing. It is essential at this stage that the head is held up and that you look towards and

The catch position.

beyond the stern of the boat; any temptation to look inside the boat – peering at your feet, for instance – should be avoided, as it will entail dropping the chin, which will encourage a rounded back. As in rowing, the shins should be vertical, with the knees at a natural width apart, not too close together and not wide apart; for many scullers this means having the knees under their armpits.

Whereas in rowing the shoulders are at different heights, in sculling they should be level at this point. They should in fact be level throughout the entire sculling cycle – and if this sounds obvious, just take a look next time you are on the water because it certainly never fails to amaze *me* how many scullers have one shoulder lower than the other. This encourages an uneven draw with subsequent problems at the finish.

The arms should be in an extended (straight) position, with the wrists flat and the thumbs on the end of the scull handles. **Many scullers row with their fingers too far down the handle, with a large gap between thumb and first finger, and this will reduce the leverage they are able to achieve**. And the less leverage you have, the less power you can apply to moving the boat. Another way of looking at this is to consider the effect on the inboard: if you have a large gap between your finger and thumb, you are effectively reducing your inboard. So having carefully set the boat up, you will end up rowing with a harder rig.

I have also observed many scullers who have one hand positioned correctly and the other incorrectly, and this will create the situation where slightly more power is applied to one blade than to the other. If you are having difficulty steering, I would suggest that this is one of the first areas you should check.

One of the main differences between rowing and sculling is that, whereas the rower is in a relatively secure position at the moment of entry, the sculler is more vulnerable at this point. This is because in order to achieve the correct angle of entry, the sculler's hands will be wide apart and possibly just outside the line of the boat, a position which *can* be very unstable – even scary! – and so requires considerable confidence. If you watch scullers on the river you may notice that many of them row short, and this is generally because of this basic feeling of insecurity.

There is no easy way to overcome this, the best solution perhaps being to go back to sculling at three-quarter slides; when you feel secure doing this, gradually begin to extend your range of movement. One of the things which I have found helps, is to concentrate on feeling that you feel on top of the sculls, rather than the sculls being a long way in front of you. If you concentrate on this whilst trying to 'open your chest out', you are more likely to be in the correct position.

Once you have reached the correct position, the entry of the blade should be initiated using a rapid lifting of the hands and arms whilst keeping the shoulders parallel to the boat. As with rowing, **there should be no lifting of the body to cover the blades**.

The Propulsive Phase

The propulsive phase should be initiated by a strong, forceful acceleration of the legs, **with the muscles of the back and abdomen braced in order to provide a strong link between the blade and the legs**. I cannot stress this point enough. If the back and abdomen muscles are not braced, there will be a break in the link between the muscles which provide the power, and the blade. This will mean that some of the power produced will be dissipated, in other words it will not contribute to propelling the boat forwards, thus representing a waste of energy. It is a good idea to consciously think about bracing your abdominal muscles as you come forwards on the slide.

Position of hands at point of entry.

Position of hands as blades enter the water (note that they are outside the line of the boat).

23

The propulsive phase showing good bracing of the mid-section.

As the leg movement at this stage is very strong, any tendency to relax the mid-section will result in the legs pushing flat whilst leaving the torso behind (bumshoving); to finish the stroke you would then need to open out the body, probably with an element of upward lift. This places a tremendous load on the muscles of the lower back, which if not sufficiently strong may end up suffering injury.

One of the essential differences between rowing and sculling technique is the synchronization of the body parts through the stroke. Whereas in rowing the sequence is legs–back–arms, in sculling the sequence is legs–back–**shoulders**–arms: thus as soon as the legs have initiated the drive, the body must begin to open backwards, followed by a strong follow-through with the shoulder muscles, and finally finishing with the arms.

As the oar handles approach the mid-point of the stroke, the right hand should be slightly lower and closer to the body. There are two ways of achieving this: you can either bend your right arm slightly sooner, or you can keep your body slightly twisted with your left shoulder nearer the stern. In practice most scullers adopt a combination of both.

It is important to focus on the right hand during the propulsive phase as it is this hand that controls the balance of the boat. Since it is this hand, too, which is closer to the body, it is also good practice to focus on accelerating it towards the body, because if this is done correctly, the left hand will automatically come through rapidly.

If your swivels are set at different heights, it is essential to maintain the difference with your handle heights. In other words, if your bow-side swivel is 1cm higher than your stroke-side swivel, your left hand should always be 1cm higher, and this applies both on the recovery and during the draw. Failure to do this will upset the balance of the boat, which will inevitably slow it down. One particular point to watch out for is any tendency to lift the right hand as you come through the stroke. This seems to be a natural movement for many scullers, but it should be avoided at all costs for the above reason, that of upsetting the balance.

As the legs approach the end of their movement, the shoulders should start to open out, closely followed by the arms. In my view this is the weakest area in many scullers: in order to have a strong finish in sculling you must have strong shoulder and upper back muscles, because it is impossible otherwise to maintain the acceleration of the boat past the blade. Too often you see the blades popping out before the stroke has been properly finished, and this is indicative of weak shoulder and upper body co-ordination, and/or of weak musculature. It follows that if you bend your right arm sooner, you are less able to use the weight of your body to maintain the acceleration of the boat past the blade. **Particular attention must therefore be paid to strengthening the upper body if you wish to scull efficiently**.

It is worth mentioning at this point that in general, scullers exhibit many more variations on the particular body angles they reach at the catch and finish position than are seen in rowing crews. Some lie back at the finish by as much as 30 degrees past the vertical, others adopt a more upright position. My own view is that the further past the vertical you go, the more you need to weigh up carefully the advantages or otherwise of doing so.

There are two considerations here: one is that it takes time and energy to go from the vertical to your eventual finish position, and back up to the vertical again; thus the further back you lie, the more time and energy it will cost. The other thing you need to consider is that as you go past the vertical your centre of gravity will become lower, and when you come back to the vertical during the recovery your centre of gravity will become higher; and we have already established that any vertical movements should be minimized because they will cause the boat to pitch, thus slowing it down.

Some coaches argue that the lighter you are, the more you need to lie back at the finish, their reasoning being that you can use your bodyweight for longer – because you remain suspended for longer – to maintain acceleration. I would argue that this can only be true for as long as your arms remain straight: as

The finish position (note the position of the body).

soon as you bend them, you cannot remain suspended and therefore you will need to use your shoulders and upper body as outlined earlier. I therefore coach a relatively upright finish position, minimizing the distance past the vertical and it goes without saying that to do this, you need to have a strong emphasis on developing shoulder and upper body strength.

It is important to keep the elbows high – the forearms should be at least horizontal – at the finish to ensure that the blades remain fully covered. Also, the stretcher should be adjusted so that at the finish the scull handles are not able to go past the side of the body. If the stretcher is incorrectly adjusted, the blades will be dragged out at the finish, rather than cleanly extracted.

The Extraction of the Blade

The extraction of the blades is performed by tapping down with both hands as the scull handles approach the breast-bone. At no point should the handles touch the body, and there should be **no more than one hand-width between the scull handles at this point**. The scull handles are then rolled, using the fingers and thumb, from the base of the hands into the fingers.

The Recovery Phase

The left hand should lead away, closely followed by the right hand; it should be carried in front of and slightly higher than the right – ideally the **knuckles of the right hand should be just below the left wrist**. To facilitate this you can adopt a position where the left shoulder is slightly in front of the right.

Just as we concentrated on the right hand during the propulsive phase, so it is important to focus on the left hand during the recovery phase. However, there is a common tendency for the right hand to move more quickly than

Hands finishing just before they touch the body.

Left hand leading with right tucked in behind.

the left at this point, and this should be discouraged because it will impede the correct sequence and may lead to balance problems. One word of caution, though: if the problem is that the right hand is moving too quickly, as is usual, it is better to **concentrate on slowing down the right hand, rather than speeding up the left**. As the movement should be unhurried, concentrating too much on speeding up the left hand will merely result in the right hand speeding up as well, thereby exacerbating the problem

As with rowing, the body should pivot from the hips until the desired body angle at the catch is reached, in a movement which should be steady and unhurried. The body should be in position before the seat starts to move forwards, and when the latter does move, it should do so at the same speed as the boat is travelling. As you approach frontstops, you should roll the handles, using the fingers, to square the blade ready for the catch.

Once again, just as in rowing technique, you should be preparing to change direction from the moment the blades leave the water and you begin to come up the slide.

Sculling technique – the complete sequence.

The 1996 United States lightweight men quadruple scull showing good uniformity in technique.

3　Technical Exercises

As with most sports, there are many exercises that rowers can use to help improve their technique. Due to the constraints of space it would be impossible to list all of them, so what I have attempted to do is to describe the ones more commonly used. However, before looking at the different types of exercises, it is worth considering why we use technical exercises at all; and I shall also highlight some general principles relating to their use.

It may seem obvious to say that the main reason athletes use technical exercises is to improve their technique. I do feel, however, that in rowing these exercises are very often not viewed as an important part in developing technique, but as an annoying preparation for the physical work in a training session. Rowers (and coaches!) often seem to spend as little time as possible on exercises, preferring instead to treat them as no more than part of the warm-up routine; they just go through the motions of doing their slidework, without any real commitment to, or understanding of what they are trying to achieve.

It is too easy to dismiss exercises as a tedious, compulsory part of a training session, especially when there is only a limited amount of time available; nevertheless they are an important tool in developing good technique. On many occasions I have justified the time spent on such exercises by asking the rowers to consider which is going to help them move the boat more quickly: fifteen more minutes of oxygen utilization work, or fifteen minutes spent improving their ability to apply power at the catch?

Technical exercises allow us to break down a complex movement into a series of smaller component parts, and this enables us to pay close attention to a particular movement pattern and to gain a better understanding of its importance in the full stroke cycle. It is also easier to identify weaknesses. In our rush to teach people to row, or to learn to row as quickly as possible, we forget to pay attention to the small details. As an example, when rowers are allowed to progress to full slide rowing without spending sufficient time on fixed seat rowing, it is very easy to camouflage a weak finish or poor hip pivot; this is particularly true with the larger, faster boats such as fours and eights. By doing this, we make it much more difficult to learn good technique. What happens instead is that we become more proficient at rowing incorrectly; thus, we perfect our flaws!

As we have said, when we break the stroke down in this way it is easier to concentrate more fully on the area in question – and this is an important point to remember, because if the rower is concentrating more fully, he will almost certainly become more quickly fatigued mentally. Many of the rowers I have coached in the past have commented that they have felt just as tired after a technical paddle, as they have after an intense physical training session. This is something that should be borne in mind when programming technical paddles as a 'light session'.

On the other hand, perhaps one of the most common mistakes rowers make is to spend too little time on each exercise. For example, doing backstops' paddling for fifteen to twenty strokes before progressing to one quarter slide does *not* give sufficient time for improvement to occur. At the very least forty to fifty strokes should be performed for each slide position, with a clear technical focus at each stage.

I regularly ask (persuade!) my crews to spend the entire training session rowing with square blades, including the work pieces, and I will not move on from a particular stage of the slide unless I can see that they have improved in some way. Where is the point in rowing full slide, if you cannot row properly at half slide? It takes a great deal of perseverance and patience to benefit fully from technical exercises, but the reward is better technique which means faster crews.

It is also important to consider the weather conditions when performing exercises, particularly wind and cold. Crews should be warm, otherwise their concentration may wander – they will be focusing on how cold their fingers are, rather than on the technical point of the exercise. It can be a good idea, therefore, to warm up first by doing some full slide rowing and then moving on to slidework. Similarly, there is little value to be gained in trying to do square blade paddling when there is a strong cross-wind to contend with.

Let us now look more closely at the principal exercises we can use to improve our rowing technique.

SLIDEWORK

Varying the length of slide used is perhaps the most common exercise used by rowers, and as outlined earlier, by considering the individual components of the full stroke we will be better able to concentrate on each one and so make improvements. It is therefore imperative that **each slide position has a technical focus: there must be a reason for doing it**.

There are normally six identifiable positions: backstops with no body swing (arms only); backstops with body swing; and then quarter, half, three-quarters and full slide. The following table indicates the important technical focus for each position:

Backstops rowing emphasizing the need to keep the blades fully covered.

One quarter slide with the emphasis on timing the transition on to slides.

One half slide focusing on the height of the handles on the way forward.

Position	Technical focus	Position	Technical focus
Backstops (*arms only*)	• Drawing the handle high to ensure that the blade remains fully covered. • Individual roles of each hand, *ie* outside hand taps the blade down and pushes the oar handle away from the body. Inside hand feathers the blade. • Left hand leading (sculling). • **Head held steady.**	*Quarter slide*	• Timing of transition from the backstops position, to commencing the movement towards the stern.
		Half slide	• Correct height of oar handle. • Steadiness of slide movement. • Maintaining body position
Backstops (*body swing*)	• Hip pivot. • Outside shoulder higher than inside. • Timing of transfer of weight onto the foot stretcher. • 'Feeling' for the correct handle height.	*Three-quarter slide*	• Preparation for change of direction at the catch.
		Full slide	• Lateral rotation of body from hips. • Ensuring that the outside shoulder remains higher than the inside one. • Opening the hands out, *ie* moving the hands out to the side of the boat (sculling).

Full slide focusing on opening the hands out to the side of the boat and keeping the head steady.

Square blade paddling in the quadruple scull.

SQUARE BLADE ROWING

Rowing with square blades is perhaps the most beneficial exercise that a rower can practise on a regular basis. One of the most common technical challenges that rowers face is maintaining the acceleration of the blade right to the very end of each stroke. They are often in too much of a rush to get on to the next stroke, and so let the pressure slip a little as they approach the end of the stroke. This leads to problems with the extraction of the blade, causing the boat to become unbalanced. This in turn encourages them to speed up their hand movement in order to avoid getting their blade caught in at the finish.

This rushed movement can all too easily last for the entire recovery movement, thereby reducing the chance of executing a successful change of direction at the catch. It is for this reason that, in my view, square blade paddling is the best exercise for rowers and one which should be performed in the course of most, if not every training session. Now, as a coach I know only too well how difficult it can be to persuade rowers to spend any length of time

Square blade paddling in a single scull.

rowing with square blades. The scenario is always the same: they complain about how difficult it will be, how they will get bored, the fact that it is not possible to row with square blades rating forty, and so on and so forth.

In my experience, however, when they actually get down to doing square blade paddling, the results are always the same: after the initial frustrations of trying to balance the boat, they find they can do it without thinking, and then when they row with feathered blades they begin to see and feel the benefits. There are few more rewarding sensations than feeling (or seeing) the boat suddenly surge forwards because the crew are maintaining the acceleration of their blades and releasing their finishes correctly.

Technical Focus

As with most exercises, there are several different areas of emphasis on which a rower can focus, changing between them when concentration begins to wane. They include the following:

- The 'weight of the oar in the hand'.
- Maintaining the acceleration of the blade.
- Carrying the blade at the correct height during the recovery.
- The role of the outside hand and shoulder at the finish of the stroke.
- The movement of the hands at the moment of blade entry.

It can be difficult for rowers, inexperienced or otherwise, to appreciate fully how much influence a badly balanced boat has on boat speed. Whilst they can feel how uncomfortable it is to row in an unbalanced boat, they do not always make the link between being uncomfortable and being unable to apply the power to moving the boat. Rowing in a boat which is always properly balanced, without having consciously to think about it, is a necessary pre-requisite to moving that boat quickly.

When starting to row with square blades it is a good idea to focus on how light the oar handle feels during the recovery phase. In truth, there is no reason why the oar handle should feel heavy – this is particularly true with sculling oars – but if rowers can begin to appreciate *how* light the oar handle is, they will quickly realize that it is **not necessary to exert much downwards pressure to extract the blade at the finish of the stroke**. Not only is

Rowing with alternate squaring of blades, ie. one stroke holding the bow side blade square followed by a stroke with the stroke side blade square.

Practising extracting the blade smoothly at backstops.

this wasteful in terms of energy, it also disturbs the run of the boat.

It is also worth spending some time on ensuring that **the oar handle does not touch the body at the end of each stroke**. If it does, it will be extremely difficult to ensure a smooth extraction as it will scrape down the body, possibly getting caught up in the rower's clothing, and this will inevitably slow things up and interrupt the flow of the boat. To avoid this the rower should focus on the role of the outside hand, ensuring that it is tapped down swiftly to take the blade out of the water. There should be no 'drama' at this point of the stroke: the emphasis should be on releasing the pressure that has built up behind the blade and 'letting the puddle go', rather than wrenching the blade from the water.

PLACEMENT DRILLS

Correct placement of the blade at the catch is perhaps the most difficult part of rowing effec-

tively. Thankfully there are many exercises that can be used to improve this.

In order to execute a quick and effective catch it is necessary to be totally relaxed as the blade enters the water. Unfortunately this is not an easy skill to master, as the temptation is to tense the body just before the catch. The key to it is to be **preparing to change direction from the moment that the blade leaves the water at the finish of the previous stroke**; and if the body is in the correct position to take the next stroke all the way through the recovery, it will be easier to change direction quickly and with little fuss.

It is important to stress again that the body plays no part in covering the blade, and that **no discernible upward movement of the shoulders should be observed**. The hands should rise quickly whilst the body remains perfectly still.

This is known as 'hooking' or 'placing' the blade. When the blade is covered, the rower should feel the pressure build up in front of the spoon and should then push the legs down rapidly. The co-ordination of the hand movement and the legs here is critical in ensuring effective boat propulsion: if the legs come on too soon, the rower will shoot his slide; and if they come on too late, the strain will be felt in the arms. Both of these circumstances will lead to ineffective, slow boats.

Achieving this co-ordination between arm and leg movements should therefore be one of the main goals of all rowers wishing to move boats quickly and efficiently. One of the keys to this is being able to 'feel' the water, to feel the pressure building up on the spoon, and placement drills are an excellent way to help achieve this. Moreover since many rowers seem to have difficulty in achieving this 'feeling', such drills should constitute a high proportion of the technical exercises performed. The aim of placement drills may therefore be said to be to enable the rower to **place the blade in the water quickly and efficiently, with the minimum of disturbance to the movement of the boat**.

Placement drills can be broken down into three different types, that concentrate primarily on the following:

1. the recovery movement, *ie* preparing for the catch;
2. the placing of the blade at the catch;
3. the feeling for the build-up of pressure.

Although they have different emphases, the important thing is that they all reinforce the basic sequence of good bladework, namely place–feel–squeeze.

The Recovery Movement

These exercises are designed to ensure that the body is in the correct position to take the catch, that the movement forwards is unhurried, and that the blade is close to the surface of the water at the catch position. Typically you would start with backstops paddling and work up to full slide. The important difference with this exercise is that the blade is not placed in the water, but **stops short at the water surface**. The sequence is as follows:

- Start at backstops;
- come forwards to frontstops;
- keeping the blade just clear of the water, stop just before the point you would normally place the blade in the water;
- repeat.

The exercise is normally performed using single strokes (but without placing the blade in the water), building up to several stroke at a time (air strokes). The essential components to be emphasized are that:

- all movements are as relaxed as possible;
- the body swings over into the correct position from the backstops;
- this position is maintained for the entire duration of the recovery;
- the shoulders and arms in particular are relaxed at the point of entry, with the blade close to the surface of the water.

Placement of the blade

The next stage is to place the blades in the water, but without causing any forward movement of the boat; the aim is not to move the boat, but to place the blades in the water using the hands, whilst keeping the rest of the body still. This exercise works best using single strokes. The sequence is as follows:

- Start at backstops;
- come forward to frontstops;
- place the blade in the water, but do not push your legs down;
- take the blade out of the water; and repeat.

Placement drills.

A variation on this exercise is to perform the lifting movement of the hands whilst sitting at either the three-quarter or the full slide position (frontstops); the hands should be repeatedly raised and lowered to place and extract the blade in the water. Performing the exercise in this way effectively demonstrates the importance of timing the entry of the blade.

It is worth emphasizing at this stage that **very little energy should be required to cover the blade**: if the rower simply lets go of the oar handle, he will cover the blade quickly. I have often filmed crews doing this exercise, and have found that they cover the blade more quickly by just letting the oar handle go, than when they consciously try to cover the blade quickly! One way of helping rowers achieve the necessary quickness is to emphasize that the blade will cover quickly **if you let it** – they should think of **not slowing down** the entry of the blade, rather than of speeding it up.

Feeling the Pressure

The next stage is to concentrate on feeling the pressure build up on the spoon, and an exercise to help achieve this is to row for the first two inches of the stroke only. As with the other placement drills, it is important to ensure that **the shoulders do not lift to cover the blade**.

With the blade covered the rower should concentrate on **squeezing back off the foot stretcher**. Any tendency to bend the arms should be resisted. When you have taken the first two inches or so of the stroke, tap down with the outside hand to extract the blade. **The arms should be straight throughout the entire movement.** The emphasis is on feeling the pressure build up on the blade and on moving horizontally towards the bow of the boat, rather than lifting with the shoulders. This exercise takes some time to master, but it is very effective in minimizing any upward movement of the body.

Dynamic Placement

There is one final variation on placement exercises which is particularly effective in demonstrating that the blade will enter the water quickly if it is allowed to, and that there is no need to be overly aggressive in lifting the hands to cover the blade. In this exercise the crew rows at a constant rating, except for one rower who simply drops his blade in at the catch in time with the rest of the crew; at this point he can either rest his hands lightly on top of the handle, or let go of the oar completely. It is important that he should not attempt to row the stroke, but should let the blade come through the water of its own accord. When the blade has reached the finish he should place his hands on the oar handle, regain control and extract the blade.

As an example, in a coxless four, the stern three rowers may be rowing, with the bow person just placing his blade in; then after some time the positions can be changed, giving the rower at three the opportunity to try the exercise. All the rowers should be given the chance to practise this. It should be stressed that when they recommence rowing as a unit it is important that they continue to place the blade with the same precision as during the exercise.

SINGLE STROKE ROWING

A very useful exercise is to row for one stroke at a time, concentrating on a particular aspect of the movement. The objective is to row for one complete stroke, stopping at a pre-determined position of the recovery. The exercise can be used to emphasize many aspects of the stroke and is particularly useful in ensuring the correct timing of each part of the stroke cycle between crew members. It can sometimes be difficult to detect small differences between crew members when they are rowing continuously, and these differences in technique may well affect harmony and therefore performance, too.

To give a personal example of how useful this exercise can be, I was once coaching a coxless pair which appeared to be moving very effectively. The crew, however, complained constantly about a small wobble on the way forwards. This wasn't a huge problem and did not appear to affect the boat speed unduly, but it was annoying. We checked the rigging, adjusted the boat and invited other coaches to help track down the root of the problem, all to no avail.

Finally we tried some single stroke rowing, in the course of which we found that there was a slight discrepancy in the timing of the transfer of weight onto the toes between the two rowers. When this was identified as the cause, the problem disappeared almost completely within a few sessions. By rowing for a single stroke at a time, with a definite stop position, it is considerably easier to spot such discrepancies.

As with slidework, it is possible to focus attention on different aspects of the stroke by determining the eventual finish position. For instance, finishing with the hands tapped down (the blade out of the water) but the arms not yet extended, can be valuable in **ensuring that the blades are released at the correct moment**. As I pointed out earlier, having the confidence to sit at the finish, holding the legs down without rushing onto the slides, is one of the most essential elements in effective rowing, and without the comfort of extending the arms it is easy to identify which rowers do not yet have the confidence to perform this movement.

By gradually extending the finish position of the hands it is possible to identify most discrepancies within the stroke. One of the most valuable finish positions is to have the

arms extended with the body rocked over ready to move up the slide. **The transition from moving towards the bow, to moving towards the stern, is critical in maintaining an even boat speed.** All successful crews demonstrate the same **unhurried movement out of the bows onto the slide**, and rowing single strokes is a very effective way to learn how to perform this movement.

Single stroke rowing can also be used to **emphasize the acceleration of the blade through the stroke**. With a considerable pause between strokes, the boat speed reduces considerably, making it essential to accelerate each stroke. This feeling of acceleration can be difficult to sense when the boat is moving at speed, particularly in the larger, faster boats such as quadruple sculls and eights. By keeping the boat speed low, the rowers can begin to feel the pressure build up on the spoon, and can accelerate it through to the finish.

Although we have talked largely about single stroke rowing, the logical progression is to start rowing for several strokes at a time, and by varying the number of strokes taken and the rest period in between each stroke, it is easier to learn the most appropriate ratio for a given boat speed. **The longer the rest period, the greater the need for acceleration of the blade; and the greater the acceleration, the more time that can be taken on the slide forwards.** This fundamental appreciation of the relationship between time spent in the water, versus time spent out of the water, is something that should be reinforced at every opportunity.

ROWING WITH ONE HAND

With sweep rowing it is possible to row using one hand only at a time. The benefit of this exercise is that it reinforces the role each hand plays during the rowing cycle.

Rowing with the inside hand down the loom (this can be done as an alternative to rowing with the outside hand only).

The Outside Hand

When using the outside hand only, it is also important to emphasize the role of the outside shoulder in maintaining pressure on the blade at the finish of the stroke. As mentioned previously, the outside hand is responsible for **extracting the blade and ensuring a smooth follow-through from the finish of the stroke onto the recovery**, and it is this aspect that is emphasized most during single-handed rowing. At the other end of the stroke cycle, the outside hand is largely responsible for **covering the blade at the catch**.

When using the outside hand only, it is also useful to concentrate on **how little effort it takes to keep the blade clear of the water**. There is no need to be dramatic at the finish of the stroke: sufficient pressure should be exerted on the oar handle to extract the blade to the correct height, and no more, because too much downward pressure will result in a high blade height, which is unnecessary and wastes energy and time.

The Inside Hand

The inside hand is used primarily to **feather and square the blade**. It is also important to use the inside arm to maintain pressure on the oar handle approaching the finish of the stroke. I tend to use inside-hand-only paddling for a particular purpose, such as when a rower has difficulty in feathering the blade or drops his wrist at the finish.

As it is more difficult to support the weight of the oar just using the inside hand, it is important not to overdo this exercise.

Alternate Hands

As a variation to rowing with one hand only, it can be fun (not to say mentally stimulating!) to alternate between the inside and the outside hand; thus one stroke could be taken using the inside hand only, followed by one stroke with the outside hand.

As you develop this skill you can progress to taking several strokes – say, ten – using one hand, followed by ten using the other. As with all exercises, when using alternate hands you should understand why you are doing so, and concentrate on the point of technique you have selected to improve; there is little benefit in merely going through the motions. Alternating between hands gives the opportunity to work on several aspects of rowing technique within a short space of time.

ROWING WITH THE EYES CLOSED

A most beneficial exercise is to row with the eyes closed. Most of us enjoy the five different senses of smell, touch, sound, taste and sight, which we use to construct a mental picture of something. In rowing, smell and taste are not used very much, leaving sound, sight and touch as the dominant senses. Rowing with the eyes closed – on a suitably safe stretch of water – effectively shuts off sight, thus enabling the rower to focus more on the other two.

Coaches and rowers alike talk a great deal about the 'feel of the boat', yet it can be a difficult concept to grasp, and rowing with the eyes closed is, in my view, one of the best ways of helping us to appreciate this feeling. In order to get the most benefit from this technique, it is essential to concentrate fully on the two senses remaining, those of touch and sound. It is not enough simply to close your eyes and expect the boat suddenly to move

better. When you close your eyes the first thing you will notice is that the timing of the blades becomes erratic. This is not really surprising, as we rely a great deal on sight to know when to put the blade in the water.

I would therefore suggest that you start this experiment by concentrating on the timing, and in order to do this you need both to listen and to feel the movement of the boat beneath you. As you listen you will also hear the other rowers as they begin to travel up the slide to frontstops, and the **timing of this initial movement is critical in minimizing the disruption to the run of the boat**; you can be more accurate if you listen carefully for the moment the seats begin to travel.

As you approach frontstops you will need to listen more intently, so that you learn to cover the blades at the same time as the rest of the crew. When the blade is fully covered and propelling the boat forwards, it becomes more a matter of feeling for the timing rather than listening for it. It is therefore more effective to concentrate on feeling the pressure building up on the spoon at this point – it should then not take long to bring the timing back to a reasonable standard.

At this stage you can begin focusing on how much noise is being created – I always say to my crews that they should be aiming for small, quiet movements at the catch, because anything large or noisy will work against the run of the boat. If you actively try to **minimize the noise created whilst reducing the size of any vertical movements, you will find that you place the blade in the water more effectively**, with a consequent increase in boat speed.

ROWING WITH THE FEET OUT

A frequently used exercise is to row with the feet free of the stretcher shoes. It can be very useful in illustrating the effects of failing to **transfer the weight onto the feet at the end of each stroke**. It can also be used to **reinforce the co-ordination of the leg drive and the draw of the arms**. During this exercise, if you fail to keep the hands and body moving at the finish, you will continue to move towards the bow of the boat, and your feet will lift from the footplate.

I have found it best to do feet-out rowing for short spells of concentrated effort rather than for long periods of time as it can be very fatiguing on the lower back and abdominal muscles.

EXERCISES FOR SPECIFIC PROBLEMS

Developing Good Balance

Perhaps the most difficult skill to acquire is that of balancing the boat, and one of the best exercises for developing good balance is square blade paddling at a very low rate, for instance fourteen to eighteen strokes per minute.

Exercise: to attain the correct recovery handle height

Only when the correct recovery handle height is attained automatically can you hope to achieve perfect balance. If the riggers are set high, many rowers will use every inch of the height available; they will be tempted to lower their hands too much at the finish, resulting in an artificially high blade height.

It should be stressed that unless everyone carries their blade forwards at the same height the boat will not be properly balanced. Good handle height can be encouraged by setting the riggers artificially low for a period and gradually raising them to the correct height.

Although this will not be a popular move, it will very quickly sort out any problems with the balance on the way forwards.

More difficult to deal with is when the balance goes off during the actual stroke. This can be due to incorrect rigging, such as when one side of the boat is rigged slightly higher than the other. Differences in the gate pitch between each side of the boat can also affect the balance in this way.

Exercise: to prevent lifting the shoulders

If the problem is not due to rigging, it will usually be caused by one rower not drawing his hands level throughout the stroke, perhaps because he is lifting his shoulders at some point during the stroke cycle. This is often the case just before the finish of the stroke, when he may mistime the co-ordination between finishing the leg drive and the opening of the body angle.

Problems can also manifest themselves at the beginning of the stroke, with rowers who lift their shoulders to cover the blade. If even one rower does this, it will affect the balance; and if they all do it, a perfectly balanced boat will be impossible to achieve. As mentioned in the section on technique, any upward movement of the body will not contribute to moving the boat forwards, it will force it into the water rather than through it. The other problem with lifting the shoulders to cover the blade is that unless everyone lifts at the same time and by the same magnitude, it is bound to affect the balance adversely.

Exercise: practising on the ergometer using a mirror

If you tend to lift your shoulders at the catch, a very good exercise is to practise on the ergometer using a mirror. To do this you need to set up the mirror so that it faces the front of the ergometer. With your shoulders at the correct height, you should try to find a marker in the background, just level with your shoulders. Having established your marker, you should then aim to keep your shoulders level throughout the entire rowing sequence.

If it is difficult to find a marker at the appropriate height, another idea is to ask a friend – or your cox or coach – to mark your shoulder height on the mirror, with either sellotape or a marker pen. Once again, the aim is to keep your shoulders level throughout the stroke: any upward movement should be eliminated. This technique is also useful in developing the ability to keep your head steady.

Digging Deep at the Catch

Placement drills are amongst the most effective means to minimize the problem of the blade going too deep at the catch. Depending on what is causing it to do this, the best exercise to use is the one where the arms are kept straight and only the first two inches of the stroke are rowed. It is best to divert attention from the arms during this exercise and to concentrate instead on squeezing back off the foot stretcher. This has the effect of de-emphasizing the upward movement of the shoulders, whilst stressing the horizontal movement that is being sought.

If the problem arises from a rushed entry into frontstops, causing the rower to fall onto his thighs, the exercise which concentrates on a smooth recovery may be the better one to use.

If, on the other hand, the problem originates through an entry that is too aggressive, the exercise concentrating on feeling the pressure build up on the blade may be more appropriate.

Improving the Quickness of the Catch

As mentioned earlier, one of the keys to improving the quickness of the catch lies in not slowing down the entry of the blade. However, this in itself is not enough, and some other exercise is required. To begin with, all the placement drills already outlined should help improve the speed of the catch.

Exercise: short bursts at a high stroke rate

In addition to placement drills, it can be useful to perform several short bursts of ten to fifteen strokes at as high a stroke rate as possible without losing technique. The mistake that many crews make when doing this sort of routine is to allow their technique to degenerate, thereby compromising any real benefit. It is much more beneficial to concentrate on improving the speed of entry at a rate which allows for good technique.

As you get better at a given rate, it is then possible to increase the rate and to **progress as your technique improves**. This is more effective than to set beforehand an arbitrary number of strokes to be taken per minute which may be too ambitious and so to the detriment of technique.

Exercise: using three-quarter slide

It can also be more productive to carry out this type of speed work using three-quarter slide as opposed to full slide. Most of the errors in technique that inhibit quick catches occur in the very last moments before the blade enters the water. If you can ensure that the entry is correct at the three-quarter slide position, you have a better chance of doing it correctly at full slide.

Exercise: concentrating on a specific aspect

As with most aspects of improving technique, it should be borne in mind that as you work on one aspect of your technique, another area will probably suffer. As an example, if you decide to work on your speed of entry at the catch, the finish of the stroke will most probably not be as good as it was before starting the exercise. This is to be expected, and should not be viewed as a negative experience. **What matters is that the area of technique you are concentrating on improves.**

It can often be difficult from inside the boat to detect whether or not something has improved, and the majority of rowers assess the value of a training session by the balance of the boat: if the balance was good, they consider the session was good. If, on the other hand, the boat was not well balanced, many rowers tend to view the outing as a disaster. However, as explained above, when working on, say, the speed of entry, the finishes invariably suffer during the initial stages and so the balance is often upset: this is to be expected, so try not to become too upset about it and concentrate instead on how much quicker the catches are.

Exercise: breaking down the routine

Another way to improve the quickness of the catch is to break it down into two distinct phases: the speed of entry and the speed of the leg drive.

The speed of entry relies on the speed of the hands, whereas the speed of leg drive relies, not surprisingly, on the speed of the legs. It is more beneficial to concentrate on one area first and then progress to the other, rather than trying to concentrate on everything at once.

I would normally start with the three principal placement drills which ensure a correct preparation on the recovery, the placement of the blade, and a feel for the water. Having gone through this routine I would concentrate on the speed of hand movement, followed by the speed of leg drive. If the routine is broken down in this way, it helps to avoid the problems of overly aggressive entry of the blade and shooting the slide.

Exercise: videotaping the training session

It can be valuable to videotape the session. Using the slow motion button, it should be possible to count the number of frames required to cover the blade. It may be that for one session (or the start of a session) it takes five or six frames to cover the blade, and this information can be used to agree targets for the crew to achieve. Thus over a period of time you may achieve an entry of the blade which takes two to three frames. This technique provides a very easy, quantifiable method of measuring progress, and it is particularly suited to assessing the speed of the catch as quickness is relative and can be difficult to define.

For example, the crew may think that they are already covering the blade as fast as they possibly can, and they may not feel the need to speed up the movement. If you can show them a way to measure how fast they actually cover their blade, it can help them understand the need for work on this aspect of their technique.

Inappropriate Slide Speed

This usually means that a rower is rushing up the slides to frontstops and it is a very common problem, particularly with beginners or less experienced rowers. It can also be a difficult problem to overcome. As pointed out earlier, it is essential that anyone who rows has a clear understanding of the relationship between time spent in the water as opposed to time spent on the slide. Any exercise that exaggerates the ratio between time in the water and time on the slide should help to minimize the problem.

Perhaps the best way to approach this area is again, to break the stroke down into its component parts – it can be too easy to take the view that someone rushes his slide and that the problem therefore lies with his *entire* recovery routine. This is rarely the case, and there is usually one particular sticking point somewhere on the way forwards. It may be that the rower is reasonably in control until the halfway stage, or that he remains in control until just before the catch. Whatever the case, it is essential to identify the point at which his technique breaks down before commencing any work to rectify the problem.

Exercise: identifying the break point in technique

The best way of finding the break point in a rower's technique is to start with backstops paddling with no body swing. If this is being performed correctly then a certain amount of body swing should be introduced, and so gradually more slide until his technique begins to deteriorate – that is, when the slide starts to move more quickly than the boat speed during the recovery. This is the break point in technique.

Having identified the break point, it is usually apparent why the slide begins to speed up. It may be because the rower is trying to get more length at the catch, or because he does not keep his arms straight as he reaches round the pin, letting his seat catch up underneath him.

Exercise: reinforcing the good technique

The next step is to reinforce the good aspects of technique, by spending some time rowing at the slide position just before the break point: thus if the break point occurs at half slide, for instance, some time should be spent rowing at one-quarter slide. This should give the rower a very good idea as to which part of the stroke he needs to focus on most fully. When he can row comfortably at one-quarter slide (using our example), it is then time to try some rowing at half slide. However, it is absolutely vital that he performs the movement from one-quarter slide to half slide correctly, and exactly as his coach would wish, and if there is any breakdown at any point then he should stop, go back to one-quarter slide, and try again.

Exercise: overcoming the breakdown problem

There is little point in continuing to row incorrectly, as this will simply reinforce the error. When the rower can perform the movement correctly, gradually extend the amount of time spent on half slide; and as he masters half slide, so progress to three-quarter and finally to full slide. But if a breakdown occurs at any time, he must stop, go back a stage and try again. As with developing any skill, the key to improving lies in knowing when to apply stress to your technique and when to ease back a little. And this is particularly true with inappropriate slide speed.

Exercise: single stroke rowing

Another useful exercise that can help rowers control their slide speed is single stroke rowing. By varying the finish position between strokes it is possible to reinforce the correct slide speed.

EVALUATING TECHNICAL PROGRESS

One of the aspects of rowing training most often overlooked is the need to evaluate improvements in technique. We all tend to measure progress in terms of the races we have won (or lost). However, although this can provide a rough idea of the improvements made, it is an insufficient measure of our true evolution since the outcome of a race is determined not just by our own efforts, but by those of our competitors. I am quite certain that most of us have experienced the race where we had the best row ever, performing far beyond our previous best and yet still coming second: is this a failure? If we were to measure our progress solely on the basis of the *outcome* of that race, our perception would be that we had failed in some way.

It is also important from a motivational point of view to monitor technical progress. It can be difficult to remain motivated, particularly in the depths of winter training when races are few and far between. If we can measure, and see real improvements in technique, it would almost certainly help us retain a sense of progress towards our ultimate goal, whether that be Henley, the National Championships or the Olympic Games.

One particular area where monitoring technical improvement can be invaluable is in the long-term development of rowers. Rowing is a very precise, skilful movement and as such takes a long time to master; I know from experience that rowers who have been in the sport for many years can find it difficult to sustain the desire to continue trying to improve their technique. Having finished one racing season, they start winter training, seemingly having made no progress. The coach still wants more acceleration, quicker catches or greater relaxation on the slide. Monitoring and evaluating technical improvement would go some way towards helping rowers understand that whilst they *have* made advances, there is still work to do in order to achieve excellence.

So what are the most effective ways of implementing regular evaluation? Perhaps the most common way of assessing technical improvement is through the use of video cameras. This technique is dealt with in more detail in Chapter 8.

The One-to-Ten Scale

Another technique is to ask the rowers to rate aspects of their technique using a scale of one to ten, with ten being best. As an example, you could ask your rowers to assess the quickness of their hands when covering the blade at the catch; it may be that in their view they scored six. With the starting point established, it is a simple matter to agree a target for the remainder of the session, or for a longer period of time. In conjunction with their coach, they could then identify what they need to do to improve their score. This may seem a very simplistic tool, but I would recommend you try it. I have used it with rowers of all levels and found it to be a very effective method of encouraging self-analysis and monitoring improvements in technique.

The Coach/Athlete Relationship

This method can also be used as a way of checking comprehension between coach and rower. If the coach makes an evaluation of the same aspect of technique, a direct comparison can be made between what the rowers feel they are doing and what the coach is observing.

One of the challenges in any coach/athlete relationship is ensuring that both parties think along similar lines, particularly with regard to technique. The coach's job is to communicate to the athlete a clear picture of what good technique is, and how the athlete can best achieve it. This involves creating a mental picture that both sides must share. If the athlete and coach have different mental pictures of what is required, a breakdown in communication will occur and the athlete will find it extremely difficult to make the required changes to his technique. Coach and athlete may be working at cross-purposes and progress will be slow.

Using the above method of evaluation can be a valuable way of highlighting if there are any such differences and what they are, thereby presenting the opportunity to correct them.

4 Rigging

Of all the areas that contribute to moving a boat quickly, perhaps the least understood is rigging. It is also a subject on which many of us have unlimited advice from the 'experts' who frequent the club bar! Most coaches and rowers have a good idea of what good technique is and what training needs to be done to prepare for a race, but when it comes to rigging, many people have a limited understanding of the different adjustments that can be made to optimize performance.

THE IMPORTANCE OF RIGGING

For many years I struggled to appreciate the importance of rigging, and how the simplest of adjustments could sometimes make all the difference in terms of boat speed. Nevertheless, having a good understanding of why the boat should be rigged in a certain way and the effects of what can seem to be tiny, minute adjustments to the pitch, for instance, is essential for anyone serious about maximizing their rowing performance.

The Club Adviser

Having the confidence to experiment with your rigging to find the optimum configuration can, and should be, your first step in preparing for performance. Compare this with a typical club situation where there is probably a resident 'rigging' person who sets up all the club boats: if you are lucky they will be able to adjust the boat to an initial 'club' set-up reasonably well. The problem comes when, having made the correct adjustments, crews have problems ranging from poor balance, to the blades going too deep at the catch.

Advice is sought from the rigging person, who suggests that the pitch is increased/decreased or that the height of the swivel is too high/low. However, unless they know the crew and have observed them rowing, any advice they offer will have a limited effect. This highlights one of the biggest mistakes made when adjusting the rigging: the failure to take full account of the **effect the rigging changes have on an individual rower or on the rest of the crew**.

'A Little Knowledge is a Dangerous Thing'

The other common problem is that unless you have a full understanding of the effect of the changes you make, you may end up doing more harm than good. Adjusting the height of the swivels, for example, can lead to all manner of difficulties with the balance, which will in turn affect the boat speed.

Although it is sometimes necessary to adjust swivel height, it is essential that in doing so, the situation does not arise where there is a substantial difference in the heights between bow and stroke side, otherwise balancing the boat will be impossible. Allowing individuals to adjust their swivel height or pitch is in my view, a sure recipe for disaster: rowers are no different to anyone else, and will generally do what they can to make life easier for themselves. How often have you seen a crew rowing along in a boat where the bow side blades are two feet off the water on the recovery, whilst poor old stroke side cannot get their blades out at the finish of the stroke: cause and effect?

Assess Crew Technique First

The final concern I have with many crews is the readiness with which they blame the rigging for all their problems. Whilst a badly rigged boat will slow a boat down, a well rigged boat will not go any faster if it contains rowers using bad technique. It should therefore be an absolute priority that *before* any adjustments are made to the boat, a thorough examination of the crew's technique is carried out. By far the best way of achieving this is to film a training session using a video camera, and to analyse it in slow motion afterwards with a video recorder.

Changing the rigging should only ever be done if it is absolutely necessary. The only exception to this, is when you are experimenting, in a controlled manner, to evaluate specific changes, such as different spans or outboard lengths.

Beginners' Boats

Although many clubs try to set up properly the boats used by racing crews, not all pay sufficient attention to ensuring that those used by beginners are properly adjusted. And as beginners tend to be allocated the oldest equipment, it is often in a poor state of repair. Thus in a boat, the riggers may be bent, affecting the pitch (particularly the lateral pitch); the height of the swivels may be set too low, making it difficult to extract the blade at the finish of the stroke; or the foot stretcher may be set at too steep an angle, which will make compression difficult.

One point worth mentioning in particular, is the height of the swivels in sculling boats.

Swivel heights have become progressively higher in recent years, and so many older sculling boats simply cannot be adjusted to the correct height without using wedges under the riggers. This will inevitably affect technique, especially the reach at the catch. Oars too, may be in a poor state: they have often lost their rigidity, or the sleeves may have become worn which will affect the pitch.

All of these contingencies make it more difficult for the beginner to learn to row properly – and if experienced rowers have problems rowing with equipment that is incorrectly set up, how much harder is it for beginners who have to concentrate on each and every movement? Whilst I accept that beginners will rarely be allocated the very best equipment, I do feel that if they are to enjoy rowing and to develop good technique quickly, they need to use equipment that helps, not hinders them. When you consider how long it takes to undo bad habits, the time spent checking the boat is clearly time well spent. Every club should ensure that all of its boats are correctly rigged, and that they are checked on a regular basis.

RIGGING YOUR BOAT

So how do you set about rigging your boats? Depending on the make and more particularly the age of a boat, there can be up to ten different adjustments that can be made. The riggers can be adjusted for span (spread), height from the water, and longitudinal position, whilst the swivels can be adjusted for height and pitch, both stern and lateral. In addition, the foot stretcher can be adjusted to create the optimum distance behind the work, height and rake (angle). Finally the slides can be adjusted backwards and forwards.

Oars can be adjusted to alter the ratio between inboard and outboard. Some

53

modern oars can also be adjusted to increase or decrease the overall length.

With so many adjustments possible, it can be difficult deciding where to start. However, although the order in which you carry out the adjustments is largely a matter of personal preference, there are some rules that should be followed to ensure the correct result. Thus, it is absolutely essential that **the span is set before making any adjustments to the swivel**, as any differences in the rigger will affect the height and pitch of the swivel. Similarly, **the lateral pitch should be set before tackling the height of the swivel**, which should in turn be set before adjusting the stern pitch. Other than these simple guidelines, there are no hard and fast rules as regards which order to follow.

The order I personally use when setting the boat up for the first time is this:

- span
- lateral pitch
- height of swivel
- stern pitch
- height and rake of foot stretcher
- slide position

Having outlined the various adjustments that can be made, we can now look at them in more detail. It should be said at this stage, however, that you should not make any adjustments to the boat until you have considered the individuals that make up the crew.

Knowing Your Crew

With the best will in the world it is impossible to decide on the most appropriate rig without knowing something about the crew it is designed for: the more you know about the crew, the better chance you have of finding the optimum settings. It should also be clear that you will not necessarily get the rigging right first time. Finding the best rig is a matter of experimenting, over time, whilst making rigorous notes and observations.

SPAN/SPREAD/THWARTSHIP DISTANCE (TD)

The first area to be considered is the most appropriate span for the crew. The term 'span' is used when referring to the distance between the base of both pins in a sculling boat. When referring to sweep boats, the term 'spread', or more commonly 'TD' is used, where the measurement is from the centre of the pin (at

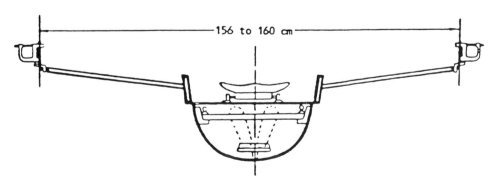

Fig. 1 Measuring the span in a sculling boat (FISA).

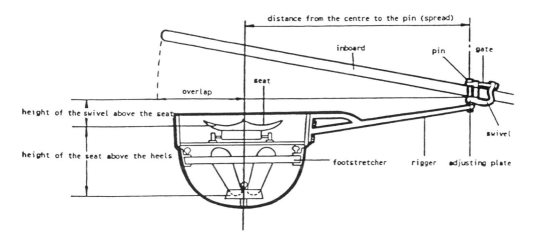

Fig. 1b Measuring the spread (TD) in a rowing boat (FISA).

the base), to the centreline of the boat. NOTE: Do *not* measure from the top of the pins, as the amount of lateral pitch can drastically alter the measurement.

Span was one of the concepts I found hardest to understand when I first started coaching – I simply could not grasp the fact that by increasing the span, the length of the stroke would shorten: it does this by altering the arc which the oar works through. I am glad to say that I now understand how this works, and feel confident when experimenting with it.

A larger arc (smaller span) will result in the blades spending longer in the water, which will, if all else is equal, increase the boat speed. The problem is, of course, that everything doesn't remain equal, because if the blade spends longer in the water you need to be capable of maintaining the force on it for

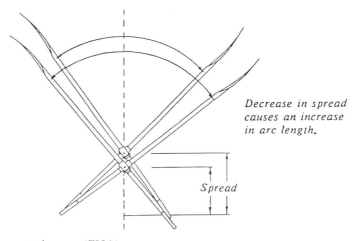

Decrease in spread causes an increase in arc length.

Fig. 2 Effect of changes to the span (FISA).

longer, otherwise the boat will go slower, and to do this you need to be both technically more efficient, and fitter.

This highlights once again that before making any changes to the rigging, you need to consider the impact on the only thing that actually propels the boat through the water: the rower. There is no point in making a change just because mechanical principles state that the boat will go more quickly if you do. We know that if we row with longer oars we can, in theory, produce more force on the blade, which should increase the boat speed. It doesn't always work like this, however, since everything about rigging a boat is a compromise to accommodate the human factor.

Perhaps more than any other measurement, the span should not be considered in isolation – it is essential to take into account the length of the oars and the length of outboard at the same time. You should also remember that even relatively small changes in span will have a considerable effect on how much work *you* have to do, and so *your* level of fitness needs to be considered too.

Assessing Overlap

Striking the right balance between outboard length and span is crucial. In practice, however, we tend to use the relationship between inboard length and span. By measuring how much the oar handle extends past the centreline of the boat, we can assess the amount of overlap. We do not actually need to measure this, as we need only subtract the span from the inboard to arrive at the correct figure. The usual range for overlap in sweep boats when measured in this way is 29–31cm, and I have found an overlap of 30cm to be about right for most of the crews I have coached.

Technically speaking, the overlap in sculling boats is measured as the distance between the ends of the scull handles at the midpoint of the stroke. In practice, however, it is calculated in the same way as with sweep boats *ie* by subtracting the span from the inboard, although as we have two oars in a sculling boat, we need to double the inboard and then subtract the span. The usual range when measured in this way is 14–18cm.

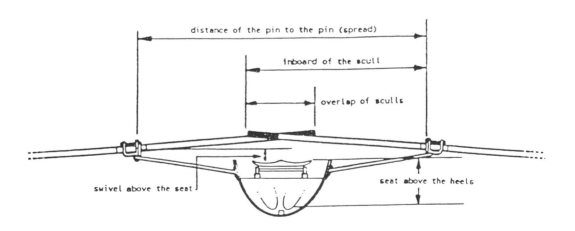

Fig. 3 Overlap in sculling boats (FISA).

One word of caution when looking at other recommendations for overlap: many charts quote ranges larger than the ones I have just given because they include an allowance for the width of the swivel. Span is measured from the centre of the pin to the centre of the boat, whereas inboard is measured from the inside of the button to the end of the oar; there is therefore a discrepancy of half the width of the swivel.

It is very important not to exceed the above recommendations, as too much or too little overlap will significantly affect your technique. Too much overlap in sweep boats will tend to shorten the amount of reach you can achieve at the catch and may cause you to lean in to the rigger at the finish. Too little overlap, on the other hand, can make it difficult to achieve a strong finish, as the hands cannot draw past the body.

The amount of overlap is of particular significance in sculling, because of the need to uncross the oar handles as you come through the stroke. Generally speaking, the amount of overlap will be less for the quicker boats such as quad sculls. When boats are moving as quickly as a quad scull does, there is very little time to lock the blade in the water and so propel the boat forwards. To ease this, we need to place greater emphasis on the first half of the stroke. This is normally achieved by rowing through a longer arc, thereby allowing more time to achieve maximum force on the blade.

The proportion of the stroke taken before the orthogonal position is also greater, and to achieve this, the stretcher is usually adjusted further towards the stern. It follows that there will be less stroke taken from the orthogonal position to the finish, which means there is less room to uncross the scull handles; the faster boats therefore need slightly less overlap.

GEARING

It is impossible to talk about spans and inboard/outboard length without also discussing gearing. Gearing is one of the most misused terms in rowing; unfortunately, it is also one of the most important to understand. So what is it, and why is it so important?

Gearing is simply the term used to describe the load placed on the rower throughout the stroke. It is influenced by the overall length of the oar, the length of outboard, the arc of the stroke and the span. There are several different equations that can be used to work out the gearing for a particular combination of settings; the most common one is to divide the outboard length by the span, and whilst it is by no means perfect, it does provide a simple way of working out the load. Fig. 4 shows the gearing for a few common span and outboard settings.

Boat type	Length of oar	Inboard	Outboard	Span	Gearing
4–	384	117	267	86	3.10
4+	384	116.5	267.5	85.5	3.13
8+	384	115	269	84	3.20

Fig. 4 Sample gearing ratios
(All measurements except ratio are in centimetres.)

As can be seen, there is very little difference in the load between the coxless pair and the coxed four, but the load on the rowers in the eight is greater.

One of the fundamentals of moving a boat quickly is for every crew member to row through the same stroke arc. If you have the situation where this is not the case – perhaps one rower is not as tall as the rest of the crew, or has limited flexibility and so cannot get the same reach at the catch – you may have to resort to adjusting the span (in this case by decreasing it) to enable him to achieve the same arc. The problem is that in doing so, you will alter the load for the rower at the same time. The above gearing equation can be used to ensure that the loading remains constant, or at the very least is not radically different from everyone else.

To illustrate this, see the example as set out in Fig. 5 where the rower in the bow seat has a different arc from the rest of the crew. To help him achieve the same arc as everyone else, the span has been decreased by 0.5cm. With the outboard remaining the same, the gearing has increased from 3.15 to 3.17, as shown in (a), which will increase the workload on the rower.

By decreasing the outboard by 1cm, the gearing changes to 3.16, as at (b) which means that the workload is closer to the rest of the crew. Had the outboard been reduced by a further 0.5cm, the gearing would have been exactly the same (c) as the rest of the crew.

Position	Length of oar	Span	Outboard	Inboard	Gearing
Crew	384	85.	268	116	3.15
Bow	384	84.5	268	116	3.17(a)
Bow	384	84.5	267	117	3.16(b)
Bow	384	84.5	266.5	117.5	3.15(c)

Fig. 5 Effect on gearing of moving span
(All measurements except ratio are in centimetres.)

PITCH

Just as the rake of the foot stretcher is the one least likely to be adjusted regularly (if at all), so pitch must surely be the one we play about with most! To a non-rower, it would probably seem that every single problem in a crew can be solved by some judicious twiddling with the pitch.

When we talk about pitch we normally refer to either the stern or the lateral pitch. It is important, however, to understand that the total pitch which acts on the blade is made up of four elements: the pitch on the face of the swivel, the pitch (if any) built into the oar, the stern pitch on the pin, and finally any lateral pitch on the pin. All four will have an effect on the pitch acting on the blade throughout the stroke. **It is essential therefore to take each into account before adjusting the pitch**.

Understanding Pitch

Before we look at measuring pitch we should consider what pitch is, and why it is important. Pitch refers to the angle of the blade whilst it is in the water. Although in theory we should be capable of maintaining a horizontal draw throughout the stroke, in practice we use an upward movement of the hand to cover the blade at the catch, and drop the hands down at the finish to extract the blade. Unfortunately it is virtually impossible to achieve an instant change from a vertical to a horizontal movement (catch) or vice versa.

If we did not have positive pitch on the blade at the catch, the blade would tend to go deep, making it even more difficult to achieve the change to the horizontal movement required. Similarly, to make extraction easier – *ie* to go from a horizontal to a vertical movement – it is preferable to have slightly less pitch at the finish. Pitch therefore makes it easier to find the correct depth at the catch and to extract the blade at the finish.

So far so good – but there is, nevertheless, a negative side to having positive pitch on the blade. The greater the pitch on the blade, the less horizontal the force that will be applied. As the pitch increases, the direction of the forces will tend to become more upward, thereby actively working against what we are trying to do. This means, in effect, that a greater proportion of the force applied is dissipated and does not contribute to propelling the boat forwards.

Although the difference is small, when the time which separates gold and silver medallists in a race can be as little as $\frac{1}{100}$ or $\frac{2}{100}$ sec, it may be worth bearing it in mind.

Measuring Pitch

Pitch should be measured in the following order: oar, pin (lateral first, then stern) and finally on the swivel face.

The Pitch on the Oar

Although checking the pitch on the oar is relatively straightforward (it is certainly easier than getting a reliable pitch reading from the blade when the oar is in the swivel), I have rarely seen it done. Depending on the make of oars you use, there will most likely be either zero degrees (as with most modern carbon-fibre oars) or 2 degrees (as in traditional wooden oars) positive pitch built into them. It is essential, however, that you **check the pitch of your oars before doing anything else**.

It is always a good idea to check the pitch on new oars when they are first delivered – you would be surprised how often the pitch is not what you were expecting. I once had a set of eight oars delivered, which were all supposed to have had zero degrees built in. In fact when I measured them, three were as ordered, two had 1 degree whilst the remaining three had 2 degrees. Take nothing for granted!

If there is a difference and if you do not allow for this when setting your pitch, you will have an imbalance. Any difference between bow and stroke side may also affect the balance of the boat, particularly for single sculls.

It is also worth checking your oars on a regular basis, as the older an oar becomes, the more likely it is that the pitch will have changed from when it was first manufactured; this is a result of wearing on the sleeve caused by the continual turning of the oar. In some cases it may be necessary to re-sleeve an oar in order to get a satisfactory pitch on the blade.

To measure the pitch on your oars you need a pitch gauge and a flat surface such as a

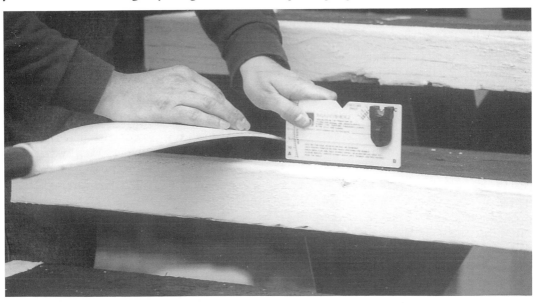

Zeroing the pitch gauge before measuring the pitch on the oar.

Measuring the pitch on the oar (note you need to place the pitch gauge on the flat side of the sleeve).

bench. Zero the pitch gauge on the bench, ensuring that it is facing in the same direction as you will use it, and ask an assistant to hold the oar with the tip facing down on the bench. You then need to place your pitch gauge across the sleeve of the oar, just next to the button, and take a reading. This will give you the pitch of the oar, and you should make a record of it.

The Pitch on the Pin

There are two types of pitch which can be adjusted on the pin: lateral and stern. Stern pitch essentially refers to the angle of the swivel in the fore and aft plane – running along the length of the boat – whilst lateral pitch is the angle at which the pin lies in relation to the centreline of the boat. Of the two, lateral pitch can be most difficult to understand.

Stern pitch

Stern pitch is made up of two components: the pitch on the pin and the pitch on the swivel. There would be no point therefore in measuring the pitch on the pin without also measuring the pitch on the swivel. Stern pitch directly affects the angle of the blade through the water: thus if it is set at 4 degrees on the swivel, with no pitch on the blade and no lateral pitch, the blade will come through the water at an angle of 4 degrees from catch to finish.

Although traditionally you would alter the stern pitch by altering the angle of the pin, modern swivels allow us to do so without moving the pin. The main advantage in this, is that it allows us to alter the pitch whilst keeping the pin in a vertical position.

A vertical pin is to be preferred as it allows

for greater control over the pitch acting on the blade – any deviation of the pin from the vertical position will affect the pitch of the blade throughout the stroke. If, for example, the pin was set with 2 degrees stern pitch, with no lateral pitch, and the blade had 2 degrees built in and the swivel had 4 degrees, the total pitch acting on the blade at the orthogonal position (90 degrees) would be 8 degrees.

The pitch at the catch and finish, however, would be approximately 7 degrees, so there would be less pitch at either end of the stroke as opposed to what we want, which is more pitch at the catch and less at the finish. Throw some lateral pitch into the equation, and it becomes even more difficult to get the precise variation in pitch that you want.

The pitch that you choose will depend to a large extent on your level of expertise. Generally speaking, the more experienced you are, the less pitch you will require. Beginners would probably be happiest with anything ranging from 6 to 8 degrees, whereas experi-enced rowers would use no more than 4 degrees.

I would urge anyone still using boats with old-style swivels to change them. If this is not possible, you should set the pins vertically and then change the pitch by using some tape wrapped around the face of the swivel. If you want more pitch you should wrap the tape around the top of the swivel, and if you want less, wrap it around the bottom of the swivel.

Lateral pitch

Whereas stern pitch measures the fore and aft angle of the pin, lateral pitch measures how much the pin leans towards, or away from the centreline of the boat. As mentioned earlier, the optimum setting is one where the pitch is greater at the catch and gradually decreases throughout the stroke. To achieve this varia-tion, it is necessary to use lateral pitch.

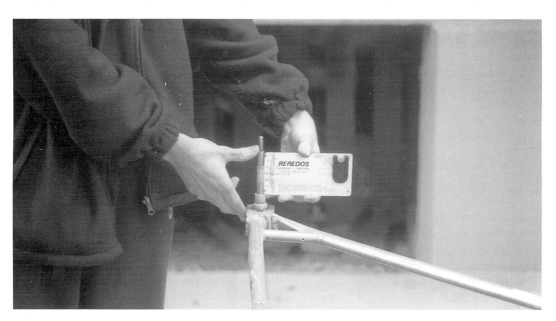

Measuring the stern pitch of the pin.

Measuring the lateral pitch of the pin.

The more lateral pitch you have, the greater the variation will be from catch to finish. What you should never have is negative lateral pitch, where the pin leans in to the boat. Depending on what stern pitch you have, negative lateral pitch will decrease the pitch at the catch and increase it at the finish: the opposite to what you want.

As a general rule of thumb, for every degree of lateral pitch you have, the pitch at the catch will increase by approximately 0.5 degrees, and reduce at the finish by the same amount. Thus 2 degrees of lateral pitch would give you 1 degree more at the catch and 1 degree less at the finish. The usual range for lateral pitch is between 1 and 2 degrees.

As an example, if you had a vertical pin with 2 degrees lateral pitch and 6 degrees total stern pitch (*ie* the combined oar and swivel pitch), the pitch would vary from 7 degrees at the catch, to 6 degrees at the orthogonal and 5 degrees at the finish.

Adjusting the Overall Pitch

In my view, the most accurate way to adjust the overall pitch is to measure the pitch on the oar, set the pin vertical (sternwards), adjust until you have the desired lateral pitch and then measure the pitch on the swivel. Trying to find the pitch by putting the boat on trestles, putting the oar in the swivel and then measuring the blade tip is unreliable. Although what matters ultimately is how much pitch there is at the blade, it is extremely difficult to measure the pitch accurately using this method.

Although pitch is very important, I feel that we are often too ready to change it. Measuring pitch properly requires considerable accuracy, which makes it essential to try to get it right first time and not to change it every couple of sessions. Even the most experienced coaches can get different results when they measure the pitch of the same swivel.

THE HEIGHT OF THE SWIVEL

The final measurement that we should consider is height. When we talk about height, we usually refer to the distance between the base of the swivel and the lowest part of the front edge of the seat. Although this is an important measurement, I believe that, in itself, it is not sufficiently accurate to ensure the most appropriate rigging set-up.

Given that most clubs do not have the luxury of specifying boats that meet the exact weight requirements of each crew, I would suggest that the most important measurement is from the **base of the swivel to the surface of the water** (see Fig. 6). When we measure from the *seat* to the swivel, we make the assumption that the crew is rowing in a boat designed to sit at the correct depth in the water. This being the case, we can be reasonably sure that, providing the height from the seat to the swivel is appropriate, the oar will be at the correct angle to the water (approximately nine to ten degrees), ensuring that the height of the draw is correct.

However, if – as so often happens – the crew is rowing in a boat designed for a heavier crew, the boat will sit higher in the water than it is designed to do. This will affect the angle of the oar, which will in turn affect the height of the draw – here it will be too high, making it

difficult to keep the blade fully covered.

How to Measure Height

It can be tedious, but the best way to measure height is to have the crew sitting in the boat with the oars in the swivels. They should sit the boat level (a spirit level is essential for this) whilst the coach measures from the water to the swivel (this should be taken from the mid-point of the rowing face of the swivel).

It can be easier to measure this when the boat is next to the pontoon; also a round piece of card attached to the end of the measuring tape makes life easier. When setting the height in this way the range should be approximately 22–24cm for sweep boats and 24–26cm for sculling boats.

Rather than trying to set the boat up from scratch using this method, I would recommend that you measure the height from the seat to the swivel and adjust this to between 16–18cm depending on your crew. A height of 16cm is the most common starting point.

The Consequences of Height Adjustment

Before altering the height of your swivel, you should understand the potential effect of the changes you make. Adjusting the height has a

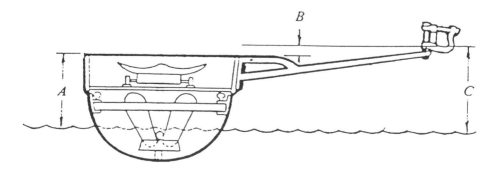

Fig. 6 Measuring the height from the water to the swivel (FISA).

Using a height stick to measure the height of the swivel.

marked effect on the height at which the rower will draw the handle through the stroke. Any alteration will affect the degree to which specific muscles are used, altering the power you are able to apply. It will also affect the reach you can achieve at the catch, and the balance of the boat.

There are many views on whether it is more effective to have the swivels set high or low. In the case of sculling, the trend has been to increase the height. This allows more power to be applied using the shoulder and upper back muscles. A longer stroke will also be achieved, as you can get more reach at the catch for the same body position, if the arms are in a more horizontal position.

The negative side of this is that the boat tends to become more unstable, and it can be difficult to keep the blades fully covered throughout the stroke, thereby lowering its effective length.

On the other hand, if the height is too low it will make it difficult to extract the blade, which will also affect the balance, slowing the boat down even more. A further disadvantage of lower heights is that the lower they are, the greater the tendency will be to lift the body throughout the stroke. Once again then, rigging the boat becomes a compromise between the theoretical optimum and what works best in practice.

Sculling Boat Heights

Opinions vary as to whether the riggers on sculling boats should be set at the same height or not. There are two main ways of achieving the crossover of the hands in the middle of the stroke:

a. Keeping the hands level, with one hand in front of the other.
b. Having one hand higher than the other.

In this country the technique taught is that the left hand should lead away from the finish with the right hand tucked in behind; in other words the hands should be level, and not one on top of the other. In theory, then, there should be no need to have the riggers at different heights; in practice, however, it is difficult to scull comfortably without a small difference in the height of the riggers. These are usually set with the bow-side rigger slightly higher than the stroke-side one, the difference usually being in the range of 0.5–2cm.

Having the riggers at different heights may lead to difficulties in extracting the blade on the lower setting, whilst making it difficult to keep the higher blade fully covered. The other potential problem is that in order to maintain an even balance, the difference needs to be maintained all the way through the stroke cycle, that is, through drive and recovery. The difference in heights should therefore be kept to a minimum, for instance no more than 0.5cm.

As with other aspects of rigging there are some general rules that should be borne in mind when determining the optimum height of the swivels:

- Start with everyone on the same height from seat to swivel.
- Check that there is sufficient room to row with the blades squared on the recovery (square blade paddling).
- In general, you should be aiming to finish with the handles just below your bottom rib.
- The shorter your upper body, the lower the height should be.
- The optimum height is the one that produces the fastest time over the race distance. You need to measure this!

THE FOOT STRETCHER

Height

There is a direct correlation between the height of the footplate and the body position at the catch. This will also determine in which direction the forces created throughout the stroke will act. This makes the **adjustment of the height of the feet one of the most critical we can make**.

Research has shown that the maximum force produced by a specific muscle is partly linked to the alignment of the various joints that the muscles work over, and it has been demonstrated that the maximum force is generated when the bones are at right-angles to each other. As the bones move further away from this position, so the force that the muscles can produce lessens. At the extremes of the joint movement, the force produced is considerably lower.

If we take the example of a bicep curl, when we initiate the movement, our arms are straight and the maximum force we can create will be relatively low. As the upper and lower parts of the arm come closer together, the maximum force generated will increase significantly, reaching a peak when the two bones are at right-angles to each other. As the gap between the bone closes, so the maximum force begins to decline once again.

Just as with the arms, the same principle applies to the leg muscles. Ideally then, what we should be aiming for is to have a 90-degree angle between the bones of the lower and upper leg at the part of the stroke where we want to create most force, *ie* just before the orthogonal. If we can achieve the same with the angle between the lower back and the top of the thighs, we should, theoretically, be in the strongest position to achieve maximum boat propulsion. In practice, however, it is extremely difficult to achieve this ideal scenario.

What we should strive for then, is to avoid having an extremely acute angle between the upper and lower leg at the catch. This is achieved by adjusting the height of the footplate until the balls of the feet are just below the seat. This implies that, for most people, the heels are set at approximately 15–18cm below the seat.

As was discussed earlier when we looked at technique, it is essential to minimize any upward movement of the body throughout the stroke. For this reason it is important not to adjust the footplate too low, because the lower it is set the more that the force you create will be directed upwards. Having the feet too low will also tend to make you drop your body onto your thighs at frontstops: collapsing onto your thighs in this way will result in your hands going down, which in turn raises the blade just at the moment you want it to be closest to the surface of the water.

Having the feet set too high, on the other hand, will make it very difficult to swing over from backstops, and this will result in an inefficient body position at the catch and may lead to rushing up the slide. It is also important to remember that the higher the feet are, the less reach you will get at the catch, resulting in a shorter stroke. Finally to compound everything it will be more difficult to balance the boat.

In general terms, the shorter the body is, the lower your feet should be. Similarly, if you have short lower legs, the footplate should be set higher.

The Rake (Angle) of the Foot Stretcher

Perhaps one of the most neglected adjustments in rowing is the rake of the foot stretcher – that is, the angle between the keel of the boat and the footplate (see Fig. 7). I

have come across countless scullers with foot stretchers that are set at too steep an angle, making it difficult to get any hip pivot from backstops. This will force the body into an inefficient position at the catch, which in turn will shorten the length of the stroke and inevitably lead to a slower boat speed. I know that in many older boats it can be difficult to adjust the angle, but if you seriously wish to maximize your boat speed, you must be able to attain the correct position at the catch, and this is impossible to achieve with an incorrect rake. I am also surprised that several makes of new boats are sold without the facility to adjust the rake. I know that having adjustable rakes is just one more thing that can go wrong, but it really is important to get the rake right.

Many boats come with the footplates set at an angle of 45 degrees. I would suggest that, whilst this may represent the theoretical optimum, it is too steep for many rowers, especially male rowers. Females are generally more flexible and so can usually cope with this sort of angle better than males. If you have stiff calf muscles or low flexibility in your ankles (Achilles tendon), you will need to use a less steep rake, perhaps even as low as 38–39 degrees. Having said this, you should aim to increase your flexibility in order to be able to use a steeper rake, as this offers the potential to apply more power.

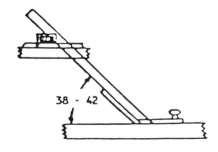

Fig. 7 The rake of the footplate (FISA).

Fore and Aft Adjustment

The final adjustment to make is the position of the foot stretcher fore and aft (*ie* towards the bow or stern). The proper adjustment of the foot stretcher is essential if you are to make the most of your span setting. Unless the stretcher is adjusted to enable you to achieve the correct angles at the catch and finish of the stroke, there is little value in finding the optimum span setting.

There is nothing complicated about knowing where to adjust the stretcher to, but it seems that it is often adjusted in a random manner, rather than to a predetermined position. All measurements relating to the stretcher position revolve around the working face of the swivel: this is known as the line of work. Put simply, the further the stretcher is adjusted towards the stern, the greater the angle at which the blade will enter the water in the catch position. The further it is adjusted towards the bow, the greater the angle at the finish of the stroke.

When it comes to setting the stretcher position it is common practice to decide on a particular distance behind the line of work and to adjust to this. The position can be marked by placing a piece of electrical tape next the slide at the required point. When the crew get in the boat, it is a simple matter to adjust their foot stretcher until the back wheels of their seat line up with the piece of tape when their legs are fully down.

However, not all crews set the stretcher in this way. Some adjust to a specific position to the stern of the line of work; this is known as *distance through the work*. Having identified the correct position, the slides are adjusted so that the frontstops are fractionally ahead of this point. The crew would then adjust their stretcher so that they could just about reach frontstops with the front wheels of the seat.

The aim of both methods is the same: to enable the rower to row through the optimum arc. I personally prefer to mark the position behind the work. Achieving the correct angle at the catch is influenced by technique and the height of the swivel amongst other things, whereas once the stretcher position is set, there is nothing you can do about your ultimate finish position.

When you get to the end of the stroke there is nothing you can do except take the blade out of the water. A good starting position is about 66cm for men and 62cm for women behind the line of work. In general, the taller you are, the closer to the stern you will need to adjust your stretcher and vice versa. As mentioned earlier, there can be a small difference in the positioning of the stretcher between boat types, with the faster boats having the stretcher adjusted closer to the stern in order to optimize the length of the first half of the stroke. It should be stressed however that this difference is not great, perhaps 4cm at most.

RIGGING FOR INDIVIDUAL CREWS

Although I appreciate that in a normal club environment, where boats are used by many crews, it may be difficult to allow every crew to individualize their rigging, I believe there are some fundamental adjustments that can be made, quickly and simply, by each crew at the start of their training session.

For example, it never ceases to amaze me the number of crews I see on the water rowing with vastly different finish angles. This is something that is quickly and easily adjusted, before or as soon as you get in the boat. So why don't they do it? Because **unless all of the crew's finish angles are the same, it is all but impossible to balance the boat**. Steering becomes a problem, as does timing the transfer of the weight onto the toes at the end of each stroke. As balance and the transfer of weight are two of the keys to moving a boat quickly, it should be second nature for rowers to adjust to the correct position. This means measuring the distance behind the pin, setting a mark on the slide bed and adjusting to this position.

At the same time as adjusting the position of the foot stretcher, you can adjust the height and rake. The height of the swivels can also be adjusted quickly between sessions (therefore crews). If there are two crews using the boat with different height requirements, it is straightforward enough to change this before every session, but how many crews do it?

With the new style of swivel, it is also straightforward to change the pitch between sessions. Each crew, or rower for that matter, could have their/his own set of pitch inserts, for example. Pitch inserts are not expensive and changing them is quick and easy.

Although it is time-consuming and problematic to change the span between sessions, it is very easy to change the outboard length of the oar. It would only be in extreme circumstances – for instance, a men's heavyweight crew and a women's lightweight crew sharing the same boat – that this would not give a sufficient amount of adjustment.

FINAL COMMENTS ON RIGGING

Before making any adjustments to your rigging it is advisable to follow these steps:

- Record *all* existing measurements first.
- Only adjust one thing at a time.
- Row with the new setting for at least three or four sessions.
- Keep records of *every* adjustment made.
- Only change something after analysing your technique.
- Do time trials to determine the most effective setting.

And finally: **'If it isn't broken, don't fix it.'**

5 Training for Rowing

If a rower is to be successful he will need training in every aspect of his abilities: he will not only need good technique, but flexibility, mobility, strength, power, endurance and speed, and it is important that he has a thorough understanding of the role that each of these has in creating a good rower. However, first we shall look at some of the fundamentals of training.

BASIC TRAINING PRINCIPLES

There are certain principles that apply to all types of training, whether it is training for endurance, strength, or flexibility. These are overload, recovery, specificity, reversibility and evaluation.

Overload

Overload refers to the process whereby a muscle is systematically subjected to a progressively higher stress in order to develop and strengthen it. The human body is a remarkably efficient machine in that if it is subjected to a repeated stress, it will adapt to cope with that stress in the most effective way it can. This process is referred to as 'over-compensation', and it is discussed in greater detail in Chapter 7.

Once the muscle has adapted to a particular stress or load, no more adaptation should be required and so none will take place. If, however, a further stress of greater magnitude is applied, the body will adapt to this stress in the same way as it did for the first, and this will

result in the body being capable of coping with the higher stress level. It is this constant adaptation of the body to whatever stress is applied to it, that forms the basis of all sports training.

Let us take the example of a rower attempting to lift a certain weight: if the weight (stress) is easily manageable, there is no need for the body to make any adaptation. If, however, the load is not easily manageable, the body will adapt to ensure that, should it encounter that load again, it will be able to cope with it.

The implications of this for training are that if we want the body to adapt, either by getting stronger or by increasing its endurance capacity, there is no point in repeating the same training over and over again. If, for example, you can lift 100kg ten times before failure, you are not going to train your body to be able to lift 200kg ten times by continuing to lift only 100kg. Although this may seem like common sense, it never fails to surprise me how many rowers use the same training programme year in, year out, without ever really adjusting the load.

Recovery

Closely allied to the principle of overload is that of recovery. It is important to understand that when you overload your body, **the adaptation to that load takes place during the recovery period immediately following the exercise**, and not during the exercise itself. If you fail to allow sufficient recovery time after exercise, the body will not have had time to replenish its energy resources, which means that when you start the next training session it will be too fatigued to cope. If you continue overloading your body *in this way*, it will eventually break down and be unable to cope with any work at all. This situation is known as 'failing adaptation' (see Chapter 7).

Whatever your aims or your level of competition, this is a situation you should do your utmost to avoid if you are to progress as planned.

Specificity

A training routine should always be designed to develop a particular aspect of your capabilities: thus if you wish to develop your capacity for endurance, you would not spend hours doing strength training, in the same way that a runner will not spend hours on a rowing ergometer – although having said this, a certain amount of 'cross-training' can be very useful for athletes in any sport to break the monotony of constantly performing the same movements, whether it is running, rowing, or swimming. In this way cross-training can help significantly in maintaining motivation, particularly amongst athletes who have been in their sport for many years; it is also a way of avoiding the damage which can be caused by repeatedly stressing the same muscles.

Specificity also refers to the local nature of the adaptations that occur with certain training routines, as will be explained later in this chapter; other forms of training promote adaptations which are more centralized.

Reversibility

Perhaps one of the most important principles in training is that of reversibility, meaning that the body can reverse any of the adaptations it has made through training. The implications of this are, that if you stop training for any length of time the progress you have made will be undone. Many studies have shown that, depending on what specific areas have been trained, the body can become 'detrained' – that is, it can lose the benefit gained from training – anywhere up to three times as quickly. Thus if, for instance, it has taken you six weeks to improve your strength, it may take only two weeks to lose that improvement.

There are very clear implications for this, particularly in relation to the traditional rest period at the end of the racing season when many crews take anything up to three months off training between the National Championships and commencing winter training. The other obvious area for concern is when injury or illness strikes, and it is vital that, where possible, some form of training should be continued – subject, of course, to medical advice.

Evaluation

The final principle of training is that of evaluation. As much as you need to overload the body in order to improve, so too should you be constantly evaluating your situation: as I have mentioned previously, if you do not increase the workload when your body has adapted to it, no further adaptation will occur; and the key to knowing when adaptation has occurred and so when to increase the training load is regular evaluation of your progress.

Testing on a regular basis is therefore an essential part of any training programme. Moreover it doesn't just give you an indication of when to increase your training load, it also allows for evaluation of the training programme itself: it is only through regular testing that you can determine whether the programme is actually achieving the desired aims or not. Unfortunately, testing is one area that can often be overlooked – but if you do *not* evaluate your programme regularly, your only way of knowing that it is working is when you come to race, by which stage, of course, it is too late to make any changes. (The subject of testing and evaluating training programmes is covered in more detail in Chapter 8.)

TYPES OF TRAINING

We shall now look at the different sorts of training we should be doing to improve our rowing performance. Rowing is primarily a strength-endurance event, and so the training should aim primarily to improve these two characteristics. On the whole it is more practical and efficient to train for strength in the gymnasium. Endurance, however, is best developed in the boat – although it *can* be developed on land, it is important to work the precise muscles used during rowing, which means doing the bulk of this training on the water.

The reason for this is that the main physical effect achieved when training for endurance is an increase in the number of capillaries surrounding the muscle. This tends to produce a localized effect, rather than a general one. If you were to do your endurance training using muscles which were not directly employed during the rowing movement, fewer capillaries would develop round the rowing muscles in question, thereby minimizing the desired training effect.

As the bulk of your training time will be spent on the water, we will next take a closer look at the various methods used in the boat.

WATER TRAINING

The training a rower carries out on the water is designed to improve his two main physiological capacities: his aerobic and anaerobic capacity. This training can be divided into six main types, as follows: oxygen utilization 1 (UT1), oxygen utilization 2 (UT2), oxygen transport (TR), anaerobic threshold (AT), lactate (L) and finally alactate (AL) training. The table below shows these, together with the rates as recommended by the World Governing Body for Rowing (*Fédération Internationale des Sociétés D'Aviron* – FISA). The table also shows some commonly used examples of each (further examples can be found in Appendix 2).

Training type	Work	Rating	Rest	% of max heart rate	Pulse*
UT2	60–90'	18–22	none	65–75%	130–150
UT1	45–60'	20–24	none	75–85%	150–170
AT	2 × 20'	24–28	8–10'	85–90%	170–180
TR	6 × 5'	26–30	6–8'	90–95%	180–190
L	6 × 500m	32–42	2–3'	95–100%	190–max
Al	10 × 15/	max	30/	N/A	N/A
Key: / = stroke, ' = minute					

Fig. 8 FISA guidelines for training, taken from the FISA *Training Manual.*
NOTE: Heart rates assume a maximum heart rate of 200 beats per minute (bpm).

Oxygen Utilization

The principle aim of UT training is to improve the body's ability to use the oxygen delivered to the muscles via the bloodstream. To achieve this the body must make several physiological adaptations, and those brought about by UT training are namely an increase in the number of capillaries and mitochondria surrounding each muscle, and an increased amount of myoglobin.

These changes lead to an increased oxidative capacity in the muscles. One important point regarding UT training is that most of the adaptations created occur at the site of the muscles being stressed, and as mentioned earlier, this makes it essential that UT training is carried out in the boat whenever possible.

Oxygen Transport

Oxygen transport (TR) training is designed to increase the body's ability to transfer the oxygen-rich blood from the heart to the muscles. Just as we can train the skeletal muscles to become stronger, so it is possible to make the heart, which is also a muscle, stronger. Oxygen transport training is therefore strength training for the heart.

This type of training increases the efficiency of the heart in two different ways: it becomes larger through hypertrophy, and the force of each contraction becomes more powerful; and as it becomes larger, the amount of blood it can contain increases. This means that with every beat of the heart more blood is expelled into the bloodstream than was the case prior to training.

In addition to pumping out more blood per beat, the heart is able to exert a more forceful contraction, which results in the blood being expelled more forcefully. The fact that each contraction becomes stronger is very important because of the fact that with UT training, the number of capillaries surrounding each muscle increases, creating a larger network for the blood to be pumped through. This results in an increased resistance which must be overcome in order that the increased blood supply may be delivered to the muscles.

The more forceful contraction of the heart is one way in which the body overcomes the increased resistance, and this and the bigger capillary network both contribute to an increased ability to deliver the oxygen-rich blood to the working muscles. This means that for a given heart rate, more blood is delivered to the muscles, and the more blood that is transported to the muscles, the more oxygen there is available for exercise. This partly explains why athletes who are very fit can produce a given workload at a lower heart rate than those who are less fit.

The Anaerobic Threshold

As the name implies, AT training is designed to improve the rower's anaerobic threshold. The maximum workload at which you can exercise aerobically involves working just below the exercise intensity at which lactic acid begins to accumulate in the bloodstream. (Lactic acid is a byproduct which occurs in the muscles as glycogen is broken down to create energy anaerobically.) AT training is therefore designed to encourage development of the aerobic capacity.

It is essential when doing this type of training that you exercise at the correct intensity. If you were to exercise above your AT, the excess lactic acid produced would accumulate in the bloodstream and eventually cause a decrease in your power output – you would no longer be able to continue the exercise at the required intensity. If, on the other hand, you exercise at an intensity some way below your AT, you will not stress your body to its maximum. In both these cases, the training effect will be lower than that hoped for.

The usual method of ensuring that you exercise at the correct intensity is to use a heart-rate monitor, although for this you must know the corresponding heart rate for your AT. To establish this you would normally need do an incremental test on a rowing ergometer in a laboratory, where the staff would take blood samples from you after each work increment. These blood samples would then be analysed to find out the levels of lactic acid correlative to your heart rate after each work increment, and a recommendation made.

It is possible, however, to get an approximation of your heart rate as it corresponds to your AT using an ergometer and a heart-rate monitor. This test is described in detail in Chapter 8.

AT Training for Crews

One of the challenges we face in rowing is that it is very difficult, if not impossible, to ensure that everyone in a crew is working at the required intensity. This is more of a problem with AT training than with other types of water training.

When doing UT training, for example, it is less crucial that the rowers are working at the same intensity as they will, within reason, gain the required benefit from the training. With AT training, however, this is not the case, and if we take the example of a coxless four, it is perfectly possible for the stern pair to be exercising well below their AT, whilst the bow pair are exercising above their AT. Clearly this would mean that the rowers would be getting a different training effect. Those in the stern would be working below their maximum aerobic level, and so would not receive the desired training effect – they would, of course, be getting some benefit from the training, but not as much as they would have hoped for. The rowers in the bow, on the other hand, would be training a different energy system and so they, too, would not be achieving the desired effect. How then do we overcome this difficulty?

First the crew itself must be considered. Several exercise physiologists with whom I have spoken have commented that, in their experience, most international rowers have a similar heart rate at AT, and so it is unlikely for there to be a wide range of heart rates at AT within any such crew boat: the chances are that they will all probably be operating at, or very close to, their AT during specific AT training sessions. This makes sense when we consider that international athletes in any sport tend to form a very homogenous group, and to be successful at that level, there are certain physiological characteristics they will require. This is true for all sports, and athletes will probably also have followed roughly similar training programmes in the years leading up to international selection. Both these factors will reduce the likelihood of having extremes of heart rates at AT within any one crew.

But what about club-level athletes? Here there is undoubtedly more chance of having extremes in heart rates at AT, particularly when we consider the way most club-level crews are formed. With the exception of the larger rowing clubs, most are put together not as a result of careful selection procedures, physiological testing and so forth, but purely on whoever is available and willing to do the training. It is for this reason that I feel club crews would benefit from testing for AT on a regular basis (provided they used the information wisely).

Lactate Training

Lactate training is designed to enhance the ability of the body to produce work anaerobically. There are two main types of lactate training: lactate production and removal, and lactate tolerance, and these need to be trained in quite distinct ways. Traditionally rowers have tended to do lactate tolerance work, where the aim is to gradually build up the level of lactic acid in the body by performing a series of work pieces. The increasing amount of lactic acid forces the body to become accustomed to the high levels experienced during the race.

A classic example of this type of training would be to row six 500m stretches, with a rest period of between 1.25 and 1.5 times the work period. With such a short rest period the body does not have sufficient time to bring the lactic acid levels back to normal. This means in effect that at the start of each work piece, the lactic acid level is slightly higher than at the start of the previous piece. As the work

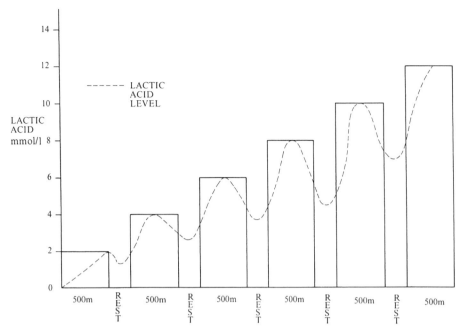

Fig. 9a Effect of lactate tolerance training (6 × 500m).

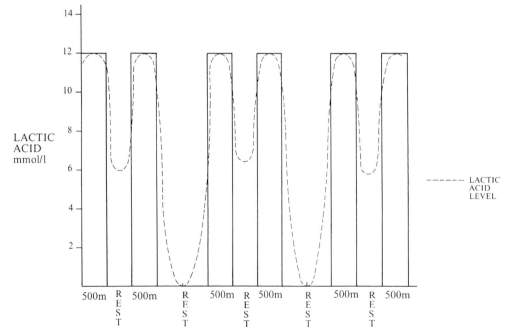

Fig. 9b Effect of lactate production and removal training (6 × 500m).

pieces progress, the lactic acid levels gradually accumulate, with the last piece being performed with the most lactic acid.

A lactate production and removal training session is similar, but the way in which the session is structured is slightly different. Using the previous example of rowing six 500m stretches we would perform two pieces with a rest period of between 1.25 and 1.5 times the work time, but the difference is that we would then do some one-quarter to half-pressure paddling for about fifteen minutes. This format would be repeated until all six work pieces had been completed.

By paddling for fifteen minutes we allow the body the opportunity to remove the lactic acid that has built up, before commencing the next work piece. From a physiological point of view this is a very important difference between the training methods, because lactic acid actively prevents the muscle fibres from contracting, and this will obviously make it impossible for the rower to work maximally.

If we are trying to train the body to become accustomed to very high levels of lactic acid, it is essential that we actually produce such high levels during our training sessions. This is only possible if we are fully rested and do not have excess lactic acid in our bloodstream at the start of each work piece.

Alactate Training

Alactate training develops the ability of the body to produce the instant energy required at the start of a race. The production of this type of energy does not produce lactic acid, hence the name 'alactate', meaning 'without lactate'.

As our bodies have enough stored energy for approximately 3–4 seconds of activity, the energy system used to provide this does not significantly contribute to the rowing race; and since the small amount of energy produced in this way is not a limiting factor in rowing, little time is therefore devoted to training specifically to improve it. Training for speed will nevertheless improve this aspect of your performance, as will practising racing starts; so too will incorporating a series of short bursts of about fifteen strokes, at high rating and at maximum pressure, during a longer work piece.

LAND TRAINING

Although the bulk of a rower's training is done in the boat, there are some aspects of training that are best carried out on land. It is, for example, very difficult to develop strength on the water.

To develop strength it is necessary for the muscles to overcome a resistance which is almost maximal. However, when a rower places his blade in the water he does not come up against a fixed resistance but a dynamic fluid which, whilst it offers a certain amount of resistance, is nowhere near the maximal resistance required to develop strength. It is for this reason that a rower uses weight training to build up his strength.

The other reason for training on land is that it is not always possible to get out on the water, perhaps because the weather conditions are such that rowing would be unsafe, or because, as in the winter, it is too dark; or perhaps crew members cannot train at the same time because of work commitments. In this situation it may be possible to train on land using an ergometer, or to use a local gymnasium to supplement a training programme.

Flexibility and Mobility

Of all the areas that need to be trained if a rower is to be successful, the training of flexibility and mobility is perhaps the least understood. Many athletes (and coaches) simply do not pay sufficient attention to developing flexibility, perhaps because they do not appreciate how important this is when rowing, or because they do not know the sort of training that is required. My own view is that many rowers simply do not understand that being more flexible can vastly benefit their rowing performance – if they did, then there could be no reason for their not seeking improvement. They can see that if they become stronger and aerobically fitter they can produce more power per stroke, with the result that the boat (in theory) will go faster. What they do not always understand is the link between flexibility and boat speed, so they fail to devote enough time to it in their training programme.

One of the problems is that flexibility training is not treated as a separate form of training but as a necessary evil to be carried out before and – if you are feeling really virtuous – after a training session. Certainly, when so much time is already spent training, it can be difficult to justify yet more sessions to train for flexibility; but if these were specifically allocated as a part of the training routine, athletes would be more likely to accept them as necessary and would not use the usual excuses such as lack of time.

In fact flexibility training can be incorporated into everyday life quite easily. It is really quite straightforward to devote a little time to a flexibility session when you get up in the morning and just before you go to bed – a ten-minute routine is all that is required, and even the busiest athlete should be able to find an additional ten minutes twice a day.

Flexibility and Boat Speed

Increased flexibility can contribute to boat speed in exactly the same way as being stronger and fitter can. As already explained, there are two components required in order to move a boat quickly: the application of power using correct technique, and **economy of movement**, and the latter is, in many ways, just as important as the ability to apply power. It is all very well applying enormous power, but if the effect of that power is subsequently minimized by the rower not being economical on the recovery, the overall effect will be a *reduced* potential boat speed.

Every movement a rower makes incurs a physiological cost in the form of energy expenditure, so when attempting to row quickly it is important that he minimizes this cost; this means for example that he should keep his head still when rowing, as even a small sidewards movement will result in an increased – and unnecessary – energy cost. Similarly, if he is not sufficiently flexible he will incur an increased energy cost just to initiate the movement away from the backstops position; with tight hamstrings he will not be able to sit relaxed at backstops and will be tempted to start the movement forwards before it is desirable.

If this seems an extreme view, ask a group of rowers to sit in an upright position on the floor with their legs stretched out in front of them as though they were sitting at backstops. If they have tight hamstrings they will find this position very uncomfortable, and will fidget about trying to ease their legs and back. Now apply this to the situation in the boat and tell me that it does not matter! Granted, it will not cost a great deal of energy, but when athletes are racing in the final at the Olympic Games they are performing at the very limit of their capabilities, so why incur *any* unnecessary energy cost? Why not use that energy to propel the boat forwards? When you see medals being lost by 100th of a second, suddenly that energy cost becomes critical.

Before we consider how to incorporate a

flexibility programme into the normal training routine we should ensure that we know exactly what is meant by the terms 'flexibility' and 'mobility'.

Flexibility and Mobility Defined

Flexibility refers to the range of movement about a joint, namely how much movement is obtainable for a specific joint such as the shoulder.

Mobility refers to how freely a joint can move. When training for mobility you increase the ease with which specific movements can be made. Exercises to increase mobility include arm and leg swinging, trunk rotation and head rotation. Unlike stretching (flexibility) movements, mobility exercises are performed at a reasonable speed and generally form part of the session warm-up.

Clearly, then, you need to know which joints are used most in rowing so that you can focus your training on these – although having said that, in as much as it is important for you to be strong in both the prime movers (the muscles that do the work) and the supporting muscles, so it is important that you are flexible in *all* of your joints. This is because the rowing movement is dynamic so a rower must be constantly adapting to the balance of the boat, and it is this process that requires him to be so flexible: for example, if the boat suddenly lurches to one side at the catch, a flexible rower will be better able to cope with it than someone less flexible.

The main joints that need training are the hip, the shoulder and the ankle. The main muscles that require stretching are those of the back (especially the lower back), the shoulders, chest, legs and arms, including the hamstrings, quadriceps, calves, deltoids, lattisimus dorsi, pectorals, Achilles tendons and the erector spinae.

It is important not only to know which muscles to stretch, but also to have some method of assessing any improvements made. There are several tests used to measure flexibility, and one of the best for rowers assesses hamstring flexibility; this test is covered in Chapter 8.

It makes sense to assess which muscles are the least flexible and to focus on developing these first. In my experience with rowers these are the hamstring, shoulder and calf muscles: the hamstrings must be flexible in order to allow for the proper execution of good technique, and I have rarely come across a male rower with sufficiently flexible hamstrings.

Training for Flexibility

So how do you set about increasing the flexibility of your muscles? All muscles can be stretched, but there are a number of simple rules that must be observed before commencing a stretching programme.

First and foremost it is essential to ensure that the muscles are warm before attempting to stretch them. This means that some form of exercise must be carried out beforehand for an absolute minimum of five minutes, either light jogging, cycling or rowing on an ergometer – whatever you like, in fact. It is also important to remember why you are doing this exercise: not to train, but to warm up the muscles, so there is no need to do anything too strenuous.

How long you spend warming up really depends on the climatic conditions and what type of stretching you intend doing. Common sense should dictate that if it is freezing cold and you are in a draughty boathouse you will need to warm up for longer, and that if you are planning to do a long, intensive series of stretching exercises the warm-up needs to be longer still, perhaps up to twenty minutes.

One other point worth mentioning is that if the stretching session is a long one – say, over thirty minutes – your body will start to cool down again after several stretches, and in this case it is advisable to do an intermediate warm-up; for instance you could perhaps concentrate on upper body stretches first, then do another five-minute warm-up, before stretching the lower body.

There are several ways to stretch muscles. They can be stretched either statically or ballistically, and with the aid of a partner or on your own.

Static versus Ballistic Stretching

Static stretching, as its name implies, involves the athlete stretching the muscle in a slow, precise way. There are no bouncing or fast movements. A static stretch of the hamstrings, for instance, would involve the athlete raising his leg onto a low bench and simply leaning forwards, from the hips, until the stretch was felt along the back of the leg. If, however, he were to stand upright and then attempted to touch his toes by bouncing up and down, this would be an example of ballistic stretching.

For various reasons static stretching is generally regarded as preferential to ballistic stretching, and is the technique probably most used by rowers. First, with ballistic stretching, there is a greater risk of injury, and this is particularly true if the muscles have not been properly warmed up beforehand; moreover with young children there is the added risk that the muscles/tendons may be pulled away from the bone.

A further reason is that the body has a protective reflex called the 'stretch reflex': all muscles have what are known as 'stretch receptors' which run parallel to the fibres that make up the body of the muscle. These receptors are sensitive to changes in the length of the muscle, and when it is stretched *rapidly* they will immediately react to this and send a signal to the muscle to contract: but since we are trying to achieve the reverse of contraction, namely lengthening, it is clear that the ballistic method of stretching actually works against us.

It is important when doing static stretching exercises to hold the stretch for at least ten seconds, because in this way we actually take advantage of another of the body's protective reflexes: the 'inverse stretch reflex'. This works in a similar way to the stretch reflex, but with one important difference: whereas the stretch reflex prevents the muscle lengthening, the inverse stretch reflex actually encourages it to get longer. It is activated by a different type of stretch receptor known as the 'golgi tendon organs' located in the ligaments and tendons; these work by constantly sensing the length and tension in the muscle fibres, and when too much tension builds up, they cause the muscle to lengthen.

Research has shown that it takes approximately six seconds for the golgi tendon organs to activate, and it is for this reason that a stretch should be held for at least ten seconds: then you can be sure that you have left enough time for the golgi tendon organs to activate.

Static Stretching with a Partner

You can perform static stretching exercises on your own, or you can have a partner to assist you. The latter arrangement can be a very good way of increasing the effectiveness of your stretching routine – although once again there are certain rules that should be observed.

It is essential that your partner knows exactly what you are trying to achieve with your stretching and is familiar with the stretches you are using. Do not attempt these exercises with someone unfamiliar with stretching methods unless you have fully explained the protocols involved.

An accepted stretching routine is to start at the top of the body, usually with the neck, and work your way down so you finish with the Achilles tendon; this will ensure that all areas are stretched.

Tilt head to side of body (neck).

Twist head to side of body (neck).

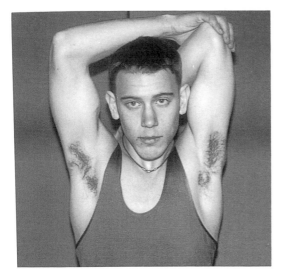

Pull arm to opposite side of body, ie. behind the head (shoulder and upper arm – left arm being demonstrated).

Pull arm to opposite side of body (shoulder and upper arm – left arm being demonstrated).

Lean forward whilst keeping upper arm parallel with floor and pushed against upright structure such as doorway or gym beam (chest).

Lean to the side (waist).

Pull foot toward body; do not lean forward (quadriceps, ankle).

Push hips forward keeping body upright. Back leg should be kept straight with foot on floor. To stretch the Achilles tendon simply bend the back leg slightly and repeat exercise. (Calf and Achilles tendon.)

Push forward whilst keeping the body upright. **Do not bend or lean from the waist.** Note the bench does not need to be high; a gym bench is the ideal height. (Hamstrings.)

Push forward whilst keeping the body upright. **Do not bend or lean from the waist.** (Hamstrings.)

Push down the knees keeping the back straight. **Do not bend or lean from the waist.** (Inner thigh.)

81

Push knee (leg) to the opposite side of the body (outer thigh).

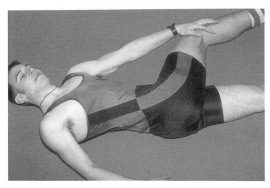

Lie on back, cross over leg and hold or push down slightly using hand (outer thigh).

Pull knee toward body (lower back).

Pull forward using hands. There is no need to arch the back whilst doing this exercise. The object is to gently stretch the lower back, *not to raise the body off the floor*, as much as possible. (Lower back.)

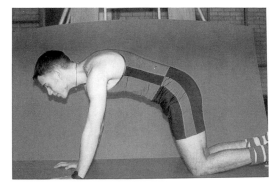

'Cat stretch'. Pull in stomach and push back upwards trying to make a 'C' shape. (Lower back and stomach.)

Arch back slightly, pushing stomach towards the floor (lower back).

Developing Strength and Power

As I have indicated, perhaps the most important type of training we can do on land is training to improve our strength. But what is meant by strength? I have heard so many arguments over the years as to whether rowers need to develop maximum strength or maximum power that I am convinced many of them (and many coaches) do not fully understand the differences between the two. However, even though in sport the two are inextricably linked, they *are* very different.

Strength can be defined as **the ability of a muscle to develop sufficient force to overcome a resistance**. Thus in order to lift a boat from the rack, we need first to overcome the resistance represented by the weight of the boat. There is generally no requirement to perform this movement quickly, and so provided we can generate sufficient force we should be able to lift it.

Power has an additional element: speed. It is one thing to be able to create a force using muscles, it is quite another to be able to do so quickly, and this is where power comes into play. Power can therefore be defined as **the ability of a muscle to generate force quickly**.

To illustrate the difference between strength and power, we can use the example of someone attempting to lift a box of work tools off the floor onto a table. We can see that there is a fixed resistance, as represented by the weight of the box, and that this person needs to lift it in order to complete the task; whether he is successful depends on how much force he can develop in the muscles which are used in lifting the box (how strong they are). The successful completion of the task depends therefore on the strength of the relevant muscles.

If, on the other hand, the task wasn't simply to lift the box onto the table, but to do it as quickly as possible, then he would need power in addition to strength. Having the ability to generate sufficient force simply to overcome the resistance would not, in itself, enable him to complete this particular task – he would also need to be able to generate that force quickly.

It should, I hope, be clear at this stage that you can be very strong without possessing a great deal of power, but that in order to produce a lot of power you need to be strong. Looked at another way, you cannot produce lots of power unless you can initially develop a large amount of force. It should also be clear that the two elements, whilst not entirely independent of each other, need to be developed in different ways.

Having an understanding of this simple principle should help you to appreciate the need to include specific units to develop both power and strength in your training programme. So how does this relate to rowing?

If we assume that our aim is to row a set distance as quickly as possible, it should be obvious that we need to apply as much force as we possibly can for the duration of the race. We also need to ensure that as much of that force as possible contributes to propelling the boat forwards. To ensure the maximum contribution to boat propulsion we need to develop an efficient technique.

Applying maximum force over the race distance, on the other hand, involves applying maximum force on each and every stroke. Applying all the force we can to the blade, is not in itself enough: we need to apply that force quickly, in order to increase the boat speed. The faster we can propel the boat past the blade, the faster the boat will move.

In summary then, we need to increase the

maximum amount of force we can apply to the blade per stroke, and we also need to increase the speed with which we can apply that force. To do this we must train for both maximum strength and for power.

Strength

Looking first at strength, we know that, as with any form of training, we need to overload the muscles on a regular basis in order to bring about any adaptation, in this case to develop the ability to increase the amount of force produced. The two usual ways of improving strength are by using weights, and by circuit training using bodyweight exercises.

Weight Training

Before beginning our training we first need to know when we have overloaded the muscles. When using weights, the usual way of determining this is by measuring the maximum amount of force a muscle, or more usually a group of muscles, can produce: this is normally done by attempting to lift a progressively heavier weight until you reach a weight that you cannot lift – in other words, until you find a resistance that you can no longer overcome (further information on this can be found in Chapter 8).

It is then relatively straightforward to determine a training schedule to develop strength.

The usual way of designing a weight-lifting programme is to determine the total amount of resistance to be overcome by breaking it down into five areas: the weight lifted, the percentage of maximum this represents (%max), the number of repetitions (reps) performed at one time, the number of sets (sets) and the work-to-rest ratio. The table below illustrates the suggested combinations of the main elements required to develop the various aspects of strength.

Type of training	% of maximum	No of reps	No of sets	Work:rest ratio	Typical session
General strength	65–75	10–15	3–4	1:2	3 × 12 reps @ 65% max
Strength endurance	40–60	40–70	2–5	1:1	3 × 40 reps @ 50% max
Power	60–75	8–10	3–5	1:2	3 × 10 reps @ 70% max
Maximum strength	80–95	3–8	4–6	1:3	5 × 3 reps @ 90% max

Fig. 10 ARA guidelines for strength training.

It should be borne in mind that these figures are guidelines only and do not represent absolutes. It should be clear that, as a rule, the number of repetitions decreases as the weight increases.

It can also be seen that in order to train for maximum strength it is necessary to work at a very high percentage of your maximum lift (above 80%). Although you will get stronger working at the lower percentages, the effect will be more general and may be developing your power capacity more than maximal force production. When lifting such a high percentage of your maximum it is impossible to lift more than six or eight repetitions, and if you can lift more than this you are not working at the correct percentage. It can also be seen that the work-to-rest ratio is 1:3, and this is very important as it allows for a good recovery between sets.

The normal way to work is in groups of three athletes. This is ideal in many ways, as it allows for two spotters to watch the person lifting, and they would be able to intercept should any difficulties be encountered.

The table below shows a sample strength-training circuit that can be used by experienced rowers; the main emphasis is on developing strength in the leg and back muscles, with supplementary exercises to develop the abdominal and lower back muscles.

Power clean	4 × 5 reps	@ 90% max
Front squats	4 × 5 reps	@ 90% max
Bench pull	4 × 5 reps	@ 90% max
Bench press	4 × 5 reps	@ 90% max
Hamstring curls	4 × 5 reps	@ 85% max
Hyper-extensions	4 × 20 reps	
Abdominal crunches	4 × 20 reps	

Fig. 11 A sample maximum strength circuit.

Clearly, before working at this sort of percentage of maximum you need to have developed a good base of general strength; were you to start training for maximal strength without having established this base, you would be more susceptible to such injuries as strained or torn muscles. In practice this means spending at least the first two months of winter training developing your general strength.

Circuit Training

Depending on your training state, it is also possible to develop your strength using bodyweight exercises. If you are just beginning to train for the first time, going straight into lifting heavy weights is not advisable, nor is it necessary, and a training routine utilizing bodyweight exercises will improve general strength quite adequately. For many people starting out, performing such exercises as press-ups, crunches and pull-ups will provide more than sufficient improvements in strength without running the risk of injury through trying to lift weights that are too heavy.

The accompanying table illustrates a sample bodyweight routine that can be used to develop general strength. It is important to remember that this circuit is essentially a general fitness circuit with a greater emphasis on strength, aimed at beginners who are just starting to train or more experienced rowers returning after a break in training. It should be performed continuously, moving from one exercise to the next, and the training effect can be modified in one of two ways: if you want a more strength-oriented effect, all sets should be performed for each exercise before moving on to the next exercise – so do all the press-ups (3 x 20), and only then move on to abdominal crunches.

If you want a greater emphasis on endurance, you should perform one set of each exercise and then move on to the next exercise, repeating this until all sets have been completed – so do twenty press-ups, then twenty crunches, and so on until you have completed the circuit.

Press-ups	3 × 20 reps
Abdominal crunches	3 × 20 reps
Pull-ups	3 × 15 reps
Reverse abdominal curls	3 × 20 reps
Hyper-extensions	3 × 20 reps
Squat jumps	3 × 20 reps
Burpees	3 × 20 reps
Dips (using a bar)	3 × 15 reps

Fig. 12 A general strength circuit using bodyweight.

It is also better to develop maximum strength before beginning to work on power. This makes sense when you consider that what you are trying to do in power training is to exert the maximum force you can as quickly as possible. There would be little point in training for power, only to then increase your capability to generate more force because you would not be able to utilize that extra force quickly enough for it to be of any real value.

The preferred sequence of training is therefore general strength, followed by power, and finally strength endurance.

Power

Weight Training

Training to develop power is slightly different from training for maximum strength in that it involves using approximately 60–75 per cent of your maximum lifted weight, a lower percentage. Moreover with a lesser weight it is possible to perform a greater number of repetitions – eight to ten – as compared with training for strength. Perhaps the greatest difference between the two types of training is that when aiming to develop power, **it is essential to perform all movements as quickly as possible.**

With the lower weights used it is possible to lift the weight very fast indeed, and this aspect cannot be stressed enough because unless you perform the movement in an explosive, dynamic way there will be little effect on your power development, thereby wasting the session. As with strength training, the work-to-rest ratio is approximately 1:3, allowing for a good recovery.

The table below illustrates a sample power-training circuit. As with the maximum strength circuit using weights, you could also add some supplementary exercises such as crunches. When doing power training exercises it is particularly important to emphasize the leg muscles, as they are largely responsible for propelling the boat forwards.

Power Clean	3 × 10 reps	@ 75% max
Bench Pull	3 × 10 reps	@ 75% max
Bench Press	3 × 10 reps	@ 75% max
Front Squat	3 × 10 reps	@ 75% max

Fig. 13 A sample power-training circuit.

Plyometrics

Another method that can be used to develop power is plyometric training which works by utilizing the stretch reflex mechanism (referred to in the flexibility section). When a muscle is stretched rapidly, the stretch receptors sense the change in length and send a signal for the muscle to contract. When this involuntary contraction is combined with the voluntary contraction created by the athlete, the speed of the overall contraction is enhanced thereby increasing the power generated.

It is perhaps worth pointing out here that, contrary to popular opinion, plyometric training does *not* increase the magnitude of the force created – it will not make you stronger. What it does do is speed up how quickly you can reach your maximum force – in other words, you become more powerful.

The sort of exercises used in plyometric training are mostly bounding and depth jumping, and these are particularly suited to rowing as they develop the leg muscles. There are two steps that need to be followed in order to use plyometrics effectively: you should:

• Rapidly pre-stretch the muscle.
• Follow immediately with a maximum voluntary contraction.

As plyometric training is very demanding, involving as it does rapid, explosive movements, it is essential to follow some simple guidelines before commencing a plyometric training programme. As with power training in general, you need to have developed a good level of basic strength before using plyometrics. Good, shock-absorbing footwear is essential, as is the use of absorbent practice mats. If you are suffering or recovering from any form of injury you should not do plyometric training.

Very good strength base
Good footwear
Absorbent training mats
No injuries

Fig. 14 Guidelines for plyometric training.

The table below provides some guidelines for putting together a suitable plyometric training programme.

Type of training	Height of bench	Reps	Sets	Total reps per session
Depth jumps	25–45cm	10max	6max	120max
Bounding	N/A	10max	10max	120max

Fig. 15 Training guidelines for plyometrics.

One final word on plyometric training: it should be remembered that there is little point in improving your ability to generate your maximum force more quickly if you are unable, through poor technique, to use this ability. Thus the majority of club-level rowers would benefit more from improving their rowing technique, than they would from using plyometric training.

Developing Power on the Rowing Ergometer

It is possible to develop power using a rowing ergometer, and whatever type you have available, there should be some facility for adjusting the resistance. If you want to use it for power training, the principles are the same as you would use in the boat: therefore just as the boat slows down between strokes, so the ergometer flywheel slows down. By rowing at a very low rating, say twelve to sixteen strokes per minute, you allow the flywheel to slow down more than normal; this means that at the start of every stroke you need to work hard to accelerate the flywheel.

If this is performed with maximum effort and speed, it will help to develop power, primarily in the leg muscles. However, you should bear in mind that using the ergometer is no substitute for using weights to improve your power.

Strength Retention

The final aspect that we need to consider regarding strength and power training is maintaining the improvements made as we progress through the racing season. As already described, any improvements achieved through training are quickly lost if that training is stopped, and this is particularly true with strength and power. When you work on developing endurance during the winter months you do not suddenly stop this part of your routine as the racing season approaches, but continue to include a great deal of endurance work in the training schedule. This is not always the case with strength and power training, though, and in our bid to spend more and more time on the water we overlook the importance of maintaining our strength levels.

However, the whole aim of strength training is to improve our ability to generate force which can be applied to the blade to enable us to move the boat faster. Thus if strength retention training is not included in the summer training programme, any gains made in strength will be lost just at the time they are needed most. In fact strength retention training is straightforward to introduce to the programme and should be considered a vital part of the summer routine. Always remember that it is far easier to retain training gains, than it is to develop them in the first place. The table below shows a basic strength retention circuit.

Power clean	3 × 10 reps	@ 75% max
Bench press	3 × 10 reps	@ 75% max
Front squat	3 × 10 reps	@ 75% max

Fig. 16 Strength retention circuit.

Front squats	3 × 40 reps	@ 50% max
Power clean	3 × 40 reps	@ 50% max
Bench pull	3 × 40 reps	@ 50% max
High pull	3 × 40 reps	@ 50% max
Abdominal crunches	3 × 25 reps	
Hyper-extensions	3 × 25 reps	
Press-ups	3 × 25 reps	

Fig. 17 A strength endurance circuit.

Strength Endurance

It is also possible to develop strength endurance on land – this being the ability to exert a large force for a long period of time.

As discussed previously, what we are trying to do in rowing is to produce a maximum force as quickly as possible. We also need to produce this force for a period of time ranging from five and a half minutes to just over eight minutes for 2,000-metre races, to over twenty minutes for a head race; to be able to do this we need to develop high levels of strength endurance. Fig. 10 illustrates the combination of elements needed to develop strength endurance using weights. As can be seen, it is necessary to use a weight representing approximately 40–60 per cent of your maximum, and for this to be lifted in sets of forty to seventy repetitions.

One of the main differences between a strength endurance weights circuit and other weights circuits is that there is very little rest between sets, the aim being to stress the muscles at sub-maximum levels but to do so for a long period of time. It is therefore important that the rest between sets does not exceed the time taken to complete the set; this will ensure that the heart rate is kept at a reasonably consistent level for the duration of the routine. A typical strength endurance circuit using weights is shown in the table below.

The bodyweight circuit shown in Fig. 12 could also be modified to develop strength endurance, by providing some extra resistance in the form of small hand-held weights and perhaps by increasing the number of repetitions.

Developing Endurance on Land

Although endurance is best developed in the boat, this does not mean that there is no place for endurance training on land. Whilst it is certainly true that to maximize the benefits of oxygen utilization training it is essential to train in the boat, perhaps the best reason for doing a certain amount of endurance training on land is to minimize the risk of developing over-use injuries. As rowing involves the repeated use of specific muscle groups, it is all too easy to develop such injuries. Other reasons for doing endurance training on land include:

- It introduces variety to the training, thereby helping with motivation.
- It can be done by individuals at times that suit them.
- It provides the opportunity for all crew members to excel at something.

This last point is something that I believe can be very useful as a team building exercise. I have come across many crews in which one member was perceived by the rest to be the weak link. Although it is perhaps rare to have a crew where everyone is equal, having an extreme imbalance in ability, whether imagined or real, can turn the best of crews into a hotbed of unrest.

If you have ever been faced with this situation, you will know how difficult it can be. Everything that goes wrong with the crew is blamed on the weakest crew member, and if the situation is not dealt with immediately it can deteriorate rapidly. Moreover the net result is always the same: a decrease in performance.

One solution is to involve the crew in a range of different training methods; then each member will have the opportunity to be the best at something. Every crew has someone who is a quick runner, so why not find the best swimmer, or cyclist? If each person can be seen to have his own area of expertise, this in itself will engender respect from the rest of the team members and minimize the chance of disharmony.

Circuit Training

Perhaps the first type of endurance training many of us do on land is circuit training using bodyweight exercises; certainly it has been a staple part of the rower's diet for many years, and it can be a valuable way of developing endurance. It is of particular benefit at the start of winter training and can be used as a way of easing back into the training routine after the rest period which follows the racing season.

One of the biggest advantages of circuit training is that it is possible to tailor the workload to accommodate a wide range of differing fitness levels within the one training session. Everyone taking part can progress at whatever pace he or she can cope with; this makes it especially suitable for use with beginners.

Although the main aim of circuit training is to develop endurance, it can also develop strength depending on your initial level of fitness. For instance, if you have never trained before or are recommencing training after a lengthy break, any form of exercise which involves overcoming resistance will help improve your strength – and this includes bodyweight circuits.

Whatever the ability of the group, the general principles remain the same: that is, to try to keep the heart beating at a relatively constant rate, usually within the range 130–170bpm for a prolonged period of time. As can be seen in the table below, a typical circuit consists of between eight and twelve different exercises, mostly using your own bodyweight as the resistance. To create a wide-ranging training effect, the exercises are designed to stress all areas of the body and are normally laid out in such a way as to alternate between body parts – for example the upper body, followed by the lower body, followed by the mid-section and so on.

Press-ups	Squat jumps	Burpees	Crunches
Pull-ups	Reverse curls	Star jumps	Squat thrusts
Bench hops	Dorsal raises	Step-ups	Rope climbs

Fig. 18 Sample exercises to develop general endurance.

The format for a training session is to choose any combination of the exercises, then to lay them out in a circuit. The group should perform each exercise for a given time period, usually thirty seconds, before moving on to the next one. It is most important that the **time taken to change from one exercise to the next should be kept to an absolute minimum.** The overall time taken to complete the circuit is what determines the training load, not how many repetitions of each exercise you do. The total duration of exercise should build from twenty minutes to forty minutes, depending on fitness levels.

The reason for specifying a time period for each exercise rather than a number of repetitions is that depending on how strong each individual is, the relative load will be different. For example, if the group contains men and women, the women may not be as strong as the men, and so may be unable to complete the stated number of repetitions for such exercises as pull-ups or press-ups. For them, the training effect of these exercises would be strength, not general endurance.

Developing Endurance on the Ergometer

It goes without saying that the rowing ergometer can be used to develop endurance – although I am always surprised at how little imagination is used in determining what sort of training to do on it. Why is it that *in the boat* we use endless variations of repetitions, sets and stroke ratings for endurance, but as soon as we get on the ergometer, we do twenty minutes continuously at a low rate? This can be very limiting, not to say boring, especially when there is no reason not to use the same combinations of repetitions and sets that we use in the boat.

One essential difference when using the rowing ergometer is that the heart rate will tend to be slightly higher for the same amount of effort. This is true on all the rowing ergometers that I have tested. The reason for this is probably that, whereas the boat is a dynamic, fast-moving entity, an ergometer is

not. Ergometers are static, normally with a flywheel of some description that decelerates between strokes. It may also be the difference in the rate of deceleration between the boat and the ergometer that accounts for the higher heart rates observed.

Other than the higher heart rate and the need to use a slightly lower rate of striking, there is no difference in the way that we can use rowing ergometers, so why not experiment? Why not do your three-minute pieces or your anaerobic threshold work on the ergometer?

Other Methods for Developing Endurance

As mentioned previously, any form of continuous exercise that, preferably, involves a large muscle mass will help to improve general endurance; as long as the heart rate is maintained at the correct level throughout, there is no limit to the type of exercise you can use. Many rowers, including the national team, now incorporate swimming or cycling into their training schedule on a regular basis. If you are going on a skiing holiday, it may be possible to set aside a specific time each day to do an endurance training session.

One final word on this subject: although you can use other sports and forms of exercise, it is still essential that **the bulk of your training time is spent performing the rowing movement**, in the boat preferably, or if this is not possible, then on the ergometer.

6 Effective Coaching

All coaches strive to find ways of helping their athletes improve their performance, but in order to do this it is first necessary to evaluate their strengths and weaknesses. When this is done, the coach will usually prepare some form of training programme designed to improve one or two of the athletes' weakest areas, whilst maintaining performance in the strong areas. Long- and short-term goals will be outlined. Regular evaluation or testing sessions will be included in the programme, to ensure that the desired effect is being achieved and to allow for modifications; and as the racing season approaches, the coach will 'tweak' the training programme to ensure that athletes are in the very peak of condition for the principal race of the year.

And when the final race is over and the racing season finished, the coach may sit down with the athletes and evaluate how effective the training programme has been. Together they would identify areas that had worked well and areas that could be improved upon for the following year.

Contrast this scenario – preparing the athlete for success – with a typical scenario for helping the *coach* prepare for success. How often, for instance, do coaches assess their own strengths and weaknesses? How often do they commit to paper a training programme for themselves, recognizing that there will be areas where they can improve their coaching? What about setting goals and monitoring their progress towards achieving them? Finally, what about preparing themselves to come to a peak in time for the major competition of the season?

Before we can set about becoming a more effective coach, we should consider what is meant by the term 'effective coaching'. The following definition is one that I feel outlines my own understanding of the term:

> Effective coaching is a process whereby both the athlete and the coach work together, in harmony, to achieve shared goals, in the most productive and time-effective way.

It is also necessary to examine the reasons for your involvement in coaching – what motivates you to give up some of your leisure time to coach rowing? It is usually because you enjoy helping others achieve their aims. You may have been a rower yourself, and although you no longer feel able to race competitively, you still want to be involved in the sport. Probably most coaches have rowed themselves and so have built up experience that will be invaluable to less experienced rowers. Very often a rowing club will ask for volunteers to look after beginners, and this can often be the first step towards regular coaching.

If your involvement is because you enjoy helping others, then you already hold one of the keys to becoming a more effective coach.

WHAT MAKES A GOOD COACH?

Surveys carried out to determine what makes a good coach generally find that he is a humanist in his approach, meaning that he puts the needs of the athlete above everything else. In all his decisions the coach should first consider what is best for the athlete, and *not* what is best for himself. This makes sense when we consider the dynamics of the coach/athlete relationship, because if it is to be a success, the athlete must place his absolute trust in the coach – he must *know* that the coach will always use his best judgement to choose the right course for him.

Athlete Involvement

The best coaches actively involve their athletes in all decisions that need to be made; and as an athlete becomes more experienced, so he is able to contribute more effectively to the decision-making process. I consider that all too often coaches fail to do this, and in my view this is a mistake because it is possible to involve even relatively young and inexperienced rowers in making decisions – after all, *they* are the ones who will be affected. Whilst they may not be able to decide on what type of training is appropriate, they should certainly be involved in the setting of the goals. One thing is certain, unless both the rowers and the coach share the same goals, progress – if there is any – will be very slow.

There is little point in the coach deciding the aims for the season if the crew does not share the desire to achieve them. Having said this, I recognize that some crews look to their coach to make these decisions for them, and very often the coach can raise the expectations of a crew through setting difficult goals and convincing them that they can achieve them. However, this is very different to setting indiscriminate goals that the crew does not share. So what sort of decisions can less experienced rowers be involved with?

I would suggest that they can be included in the making of many day-to-day decisions. As an example, I coached a Junior sixteen crew some years ago and outlined the areas of technique on which I felt they needed to focus over the coming months. I then asked them to agree with me appropriate targets to be achieved by the end of each week, and they then looked at the individual training sessions and set their own targets for these. With some guidance from me, they came up with perfectly reasonable targets – if anything, these tended to be too ambitious! They suggested, for instance, that they could progress from being unable to balance the boat for more than two or three strokes at a time, to being able to balance it continuously for 1,500 metres – all within three sessions. I make that 500 metres per session!

This example highlights an important point: that involving your rowers in the decision-making process does *not* necessarily mean that as a coach you are relinquishing control. In fact what you are doing is letting them control their own destiny, and with your guidance they should be better able to specify and attain their targets. Surely that is a good thing!

Allocating Responsibility

When rowers are involved in making decisions, I have found that problems of persistent lateness or bad 'attitude', whilst they do not disappear completely, are radically reduced. If they have helped to set the goals and have been involved in constructing the programme to achieve them, they are more likely to want to ensure a successful outcome.

This is similar to the stratagem of allocating responsibility to a rower for a particular aspect of the training programme, in order to overcome the problem of 'attitude'. I have used this ploy with athletes who are persistently late, with perpetual complainers, and with those who feel they are better than the rest of the crew. By making a person responsible for something, you encourage him to feel a part of the project, and to feel also that he has a direct influence on the eventual outcome. This is true whether we are talking about a project at work, or in preparing a crew for a race. Moreover if everyone in a crew has an area of responsibility, they are all encouraged to feel part of a team, striving to achieve a mutual goal. This will foster a climate of interdependence and respect for the abilities of the other crew members. Working together as a team is something we often take for granted, but it is a very real skill and one that can generally be improved upon.

Most coaches (and rowers) are only too familiar with the problems created when there is a lack of harmony within a crew, and a great deal of time and energy can be spent trying to smooth out relations between different crew members. This is time that should be devoted to moving the boat quickly, not wasted on some silly point of little consequence, such as whether or not a crew member turned up ten minutes late for a training session. In fact, if you were to add up the time that some crews spend arguing with the rower who was late, and compare it with the time lost as a result of their lateness, you would almost certainly find that more time had been lost arguing about it.

Involving the Cox

When referring to 'the crew', I include the cox in this. The cox can, and should be an invaluable, integral part of the team; unfortunately he is often the scapegoat for a great deal of conflict. It is too easy for a crew – or a coach – to blame the cox for the slightest problem within the boat – but why, for instance, is the balance always the cox's fault?

Part of the problem is that crew members do not always understand or value the contribution that the cox makes to the crew. In some ways this is made worse by the fact that it can be difficult to find good coxes – and on the face of it, who would want to be a cox? Sitting for hours in a cramped little space getting soaked, either by the rain or from the 'precise' bladework of the crew, suffering endless abuse and getting the blame for everything, from the balance of the boat to the fact that the race was lost by ten lengths because your steering was terrible (this over a straight 500m course)?

Nevertheless, just as the rowers can benefit from being given responsibility for certain aspects of training, so too can the cox – and I don't just mean the usual tasks such as getting the blades down and washing the boat, but in other areas such as suggesting race tactics, supervising land training sessions and logistical arrangements. There is no reason why a reasonably competent cox should not supervise land training sessions, or at least help to do so. Whether it is circuit training, or training on the ergometer, the cox can be of great help to the coach.

For example when running circuit training, I might ask the cox to do the timing, or to call out the station changes, or record repetitions. He can also help by encouraging good technique when the rowers are doing weight training; it is far easier to monitor and correct technique with an assistant than it is on your own. All of these activities will encourage the crew to value the contribution of the cox.

Rowers are only human, and when for instance they realize that by correcting their technique on the ergometer the cox can help them achieve a better score, they will be more inclined to listen when he gives them instructions in the boat.

Coaching on the Ergometer

This subject raises an important point: why do so many coaches allow their rowers to train unsupervised on the ergometer? When you consider how many hours are spent training in this way these days, it is astonishing that more coaches do not spend more time teaching their rowers how to use one properly. How can we expect rowers to improve their rowing on the water, if every time they train on the ergometer they are allowed to row as they wish?

Many areas of technique in the boat can be improved upon using the ergometer. If, for example, you are working on the correct sequence of opening the body angle in the boat, there is no reason why this cannot also be practised when using the ergometer.

However, if you wish to improve an area of technique, it is necessary to perform the correct movement repeatedly, and to minimize the time spent performing it incorrectly. If we allow our rowers to concentrate on the correctness of the movement *only* when they are rowing in the boat and *not* when they are using the ergometer, we will just be prolonging the time they will need to perform it correctly. I would encourage all coaches to supervise at least some of the sessions on the ergometer (or train the cox to do so) to ensure that their rowers are rowing properly.

THE QUALITIES OF SUCCESS

We have already mentioned that good coaches are humanist in their approach, putting the needs of their athletes first, but what other characteristics do top class coaches share? Some common traits are that they tend to be very well organized, they know very clearly what their goals are, they are able to inspire others to follow their lead, to think and act positively, and to pay attention to detail, and they are very persistent.

When we examine these characteristics it is easy to see why they are important factors in coaching success. With the best will in the world, it is difficult to be successful at something if you do not identify your goals, create a plan of action to achieve them and persist until you reach them. Along the route you may come across adversity and so will need to remain positive. Paying attention to the smallest details will help to ensure that time is not wasted on unnecessary factors. What is particularly interesting is that all of the above are equally applicable to successful athletes.

Perhaps the only factor that sets the coach apart from the athletes is the ability to inspire others to follow his lead – although a great many successful athletes also have this ability in abundance.

We can now look a little more closely at the characteristics required for success as a coach. Each of us has a unique combination of the ingredients for success: some of us may be better at planning, whilst others may be more persistent or may pay more attention to detail. What unites us, however, is our ability to improve upon what we naturally possess.

Recognizing our Strengths and Weaknesses

We are not all going to enjoy planning everything down to the last detail, nor can we *all* be positive every minute of the day as some appear to be. It is important to recognize that we are bound to have our own strengths and weaknesses, just as rowers do; we will be better at some things than we are at others – that is only human. What we should try to do, however, is to **become the best we possibly can in as many areas as we can**.

First we must be honest with ourselves, and critically analyse what our weak points are, whilst recognizing those areas where we are strong. One way to do this is to draw up a list of questions which relate to the various areas involved in coaching, and give yourself a mark out of ten for each of them.

If you really wanted to assess your abilities you could ask your rowers to fill out another form and compare the results. Having done this myself, I know that others often perceive our strengths and weaknesses differently to the way we perceive them ourselves. It may be that what you see as a real strength, your rowers feel could be improved upon; after all, it is only human to be unwilling to admit to weaknesses – the reverse could just as easily be the case. You might consider any of the following questions:

- How organized am I in the following areas: writing the training programme in advance, organizing who rows with whom each session, making travel arrangements?
- Do I use positive talk a great deal, or do I focus on the negative aspects?
- How easily do I accept a situation as being unalterable, for example, a rower's technique?
- Do I have clear, identifiable goals?

Having completed your questionnaire, you should have a better idea of where your strengths and weaknesses are, and be able to draw up a training programme of your own.

Many of the skills required for success in coaching can be learned by attending a training course. Many of these are run by such organizations as the Amateur Rowing Association, the National Coaching Foundation and local colleges of education. But what can be done if you have neither the time nor the resources to attend college? In the next section we shall look at various ways of improving your ability as a coach without having to attend any course.

The Importance of Planning and Preparation

Perhaps the easiest and quickest way of improving your coaching is to look at the area of planning and preparation. There is no great secret to proper planning, but there are several steps that can help make it as painless a process as possible.

When coaches talk about planning and preparation, they tend to think in terms of the training programme, and whilst this is an essential part of the planning process, it is only one element in the overall strategy. (For more information on constructing a training programme, see Chapter 7.)

There are many different elements which need to be considered when preparing your plan for success. It is usual to start by setting out the long-, medium- and short-term goals for the project: it may be that the long-term goal is competing in a particular regatta, such as the World Championships or Henley Royal Regatta; medium-term goals could be intermediate regattas, while short-term goals might be certain technical improvements for the crew and individuals.

Long-Term Goals

In my experience most coaches and crews can tell you what their long-term goals are, some of the most common being to win a medal at Henley or at the National or World Championships. Some are able to say what their medium-term goals are, quoting such things as becoming stronger or closing the gap between themselves and another crew. Very few, however, can outline what their short-term goals are.

This is a crucial difference between top performers and less successful ones; it is also one of the areas where coaches and crews have the most to gain, and it is relatively straight-forward to do.

Setting Short-Term Goals

So how do you set about creating short-term goals? You must first examine what is understood by the term 'short term': is it a month, six months or a racing season?

In practice, short-term objectives tend to be used for monitoring and setting goals for improvements in technique. This suggests that they can range in length from one session to a whole month, depending on the nature of the change in technique required. If we take the example of a rower who needs to improve the quickness of his hands at the catch, we can see that there are several areas that need to be considered before setting a short-term goal.

We must first find a method of assessing how quickly they are currently covering the blade. This achieved, we need to determine what would be a reasonable target to aim for. And having set the target and found a method of measuring, we then need to determine the best way of attaining the required goal. This will involve setting smaller, intermediate targets, and as can be seen from this example, short-term goals can be as small as targets for an individual session. When viewed in this way it is easy to understand why many rowers might gain a great deal from setting specific short-term goals.

From a coaching point of view the setting of individual goals for each session has many advantages. One of the main tasks that falls to a coach is to help athletes improve their performance by advising them on how to improve their technique. By identifying ways of assessing that improvement and measuring it on a regular basis we help them remain positive and focused on the task. And if we can help a rower to remain focused on his technique for a greater percentage of the training time, we should see a more rapid improvement in his technique.

Being Organized

In sport the coach needs to be very well organized, not just to succeed, but perhaps just as importantly, to minimize the chance of failure.

When we describe people as being 'well organized', we imply that they appear to be in control of events; they rarely seem to be 'caught out' or surprised by any eventuality. In fact there is no secret to being well organized: very few things happen *totally* unexpectedly, and many things can be, if not exactly foreseen, certainly anticipated. The key to remaining in control of events is to anticipate what may happen, and to have strategies to cope with them should they arise. (This topic is covered in more detail in Chapter 9.)

Expect the Unexpected

A guiding principle for all coaches should be expecting the unexpected to happen. Examples in rowing are being within one month of the Head of The River Race and having at least half the crew catch the flu; racing into a blazing head- or cross-wind at Nottingham, or meeting the eventual winners of the event in the first round at Henley. Some may argue that these eventualities are not exactly unexpected – but how many times do we let them upset and annoy us? These things happen so it makes sense to have strategies to cope with them, and this is all part of the skill of being well organized.

Good organizational skills are also evident

in successful athletes, who must be able to juggle the various commitments that they have, without letting them impinge on training; this takes a lot of organization. Successful athletes will arrange all aspects of their lives around the need to train. This extends even to personal relationships, where girl- or boyfriends become involved in supporting the athlete. If an athlete is training seven days a week, he will find it invaluable to have someone else take care of the domestic details such as the shopping, laundry and so forth. Whilst this may sound mercenary, it is a fact that cannot be avoided.

POSITIVE ACTING AND THINKING

Being able to think and act positively is one of the most crucial ingredients a good coach should possess. Some people are able to find positive aspects in even the most desperate of situations; others need to work hard at it.

One of the main goals a coach should aim for is to **create a positive environment for improvement**. This is not at all difficult if you follow a few guidelines:

- Keep things in perspective.
- Use positive language when giving instructions.
- Always remember that the athletes are trying their hardest to improve.
- Be prepared for the unexpected and have strategies to cope with them.
- Set high standards for yourself and your athletes.
- Give your crew the opportunity to impress you.
- Place the needs of the athletes before your own.

Being positive and giving positive feedback

are both very real skills that can be learned. Let us now consider these in more detail.

Keeping Things in Perspective

A key factor is to keep everything in perspective; and always try to find something positive in every situation: no matter how bad an outing was, or how badly the crew rowed in the race, there must always be something that made it worthwhile. I admit that sometimes it is extremely hard to think what that may be, but there are ways.

During the middle of winter training when the rain is pouring down, there are white horses on the water, the crew's fingers are numb with cold and you are doing ninety minutes of oxygen utilization training, the summer may seem a long way away – but each stroke they take will put them one stroke in front of their opponents at Henley.

Positive Talk

Everything you say and do as a coach has a direct effect on the members of the crew. Thus if you say something negative, the crew will respond in a negative way; on the other hand, **if you say something positive they will respond positively**. Even the most experienced and seemingly confident of athletes will look to you for support from time to time. Also a crew will assess everything you do and say, however insignificant, and try to read some message into it, and this is why a coach should try to be as unambiguous as possible. When you are trying to get across a message, athletes will very often interpret it in different ways – so you send what you think is one message, but it is received with eight different meanings.

Again, using positive language is another way of creating the best environment for improvement. If we take a typical coaching session and look at some of the instructions we give our rowers, we will see that we do *not* always use language in a positive way. For instance, we may tell the crew 'not to rush their slides', or 'not to be so hard at the catch'; or we might say 'Don't beat the stroke person in', or 'Don't lift your shoulders at the catch'. But if you stop for a moment and analyse what you are saying, you will see that rather than helping the crew to perform the *correct* movement, you are simply reinforcing what is wrong.

Using words such as 'rush', 'lift' and 'hard' repeatedly, places them in the subconscious of the athlete. This has a negative effect, and what you should try to do instead is to place the *correct* words in the athlete's subconscious, words such as 'slow', 'quiet', 'controlled', rhythm' and 'relaxed'.

In a similar way, whenever we use the words 'do not' or 'don't' the athletes will inevitably ask 'why?' and 'what do you want me to do instead?'. The good coach should have a very clear understanding as to why he wishes the athlete to change an element of his technique, and should be able to explain this to him.

The second question is fundamental to effective coaching, because in effect the athlete is **asking for your help**: it means he has placed his faith in your ability to help him perform better. By concentrating on what it is we want him to do, we will be better able to help him achieve the desired change.

Using Parts of the Body

I have found that by focusing on the various parts of the body and thinking what it is I want them to do differently, it is easier for me to give positive commands to my athletes. For example, if we want them to be quicker at the catch, we must first ask ourselves how they might achieve this – what they should do in order to have a quicker catch. Simply telling

them to be quicker will not necessarily result in a quicker catch; so how *do* we help them achieve it?

To start with, they need to ensure that the blade is close enough to the water at the point of entry. And how is this achieved? By ensuring that they carry the blade at the correct height from the finish of the previous stroke. In this case we might ask them to row with square blades, concentrating on having a loose and relaxed hold of the handle, whilst carrying the blade at the correct height. We would want them to speed up the entry of the blade to the water, and this means they would need to increase the speed with which they lifted their hands.

We might want to decrease the time it takes for the blade to get 'locked on', and in order to do this they would need to increase the speed with which they pushed down their legs against the stretcher.

These are simple instructions but they will be much more effective in helping the rower to speed up his catch than simply telling him to be quicker. This is just one example of using positive instructions, and it may be useful to analyse some of the instructions *you* use regularly, to see if they can be made more positive.

Avoid Finding Fault

When I am coaching I never refer to 'faults': the word 'fault' implies that something is broken and needs to be mended, and this is simply not the case with rowers who are trying to improve their technique. Nothing is broken: what you *do* have, is an athlete who has reached a certain point in the continuum of learning to row efficiently. My preferred term therefore is to talk about **areas for improvement**.

Although helping a rower to improve his technique must necessarily involve identifying those areas that require improvement, our job as a coach is to facilitate that improvement in the most effective way possible, and the best way of doing this is by **encouraging** him. Thus overt criticism has no place in the relationship between rower and coach: if you are working as a team towards the same goals, criticism is not an appropriate form of communication.

Letting your Athletes Impress You

Fundamental to the coach/athlete relationship is the fact that athletes are constantly trying to impress their coach with their performance – and it is very easy for us coaches to become so bogged down in finding fault with rowers' technique, that we forget to praise them. In fact some coaches seem to take a pride in finding as many faults as possible with their rowers. I think one of the reasons for this is that they see international crews displaying apparently perfect technique, but fail to perceive the fine details that an international rower is working hard to try and improve; they genuinely believe that the more faults they can find in their crews, the better they must be as a coach.

Giving your athletes the opportunity to impress you can be a very powerful motivational tool, and it doesn't need to be about winning races. Although winning is very gratifying for both coach and athlete, the opportunity to do so does not come along that frequently – the other problem being that the outcome of any race depends on the performance of others. In fact it is far better to allow the rowers to impress you with their technique during normal training. A simple example is to try and **finish every outing on a positive note**: thus, all crews try that bit harder when they are being watched by others, so why not capitalize on this by finishing every session with a row past the clubhouse?

Also, if the last work piece of a training session was not as good as it might have been, I have often asked the crew to do an additional shorter piece, not to punish them, but to give them the opportunity to finish the session on a positive note. In a similar way it is essential that they do not finish the work and then row sloppily back to the clubhouse.

On occasion it is enough simply to ask the crew to show you how well they can row, to show you how much they have learned and progressed. If you set high standards, the crew will raise their expectations of themselves, thereby accelerating the progress made towards achieving their goals.

Rowers do not enjoy Rowing Badly!

When the team is going through a difficult time, they will look to the coach for guidance and support. It is important to understand that things do not always go to plan: perhaps sessions are being constantly ruined by bad weather or other water users; it may be getting close to a selection trial or a major event; or perhaps the crew are just tired as a result of the amount of training they are doing. Some of the crew members may be sitting important exams. Sometimes, for no reason at all, things will go badly for a time. We have all experienced the session where no matter how hard we try the boat will not run properly; there isn't always a reason for this – it just happens. Now, we don't always have control over events, but what we *can* do is **control the way we respond to them**.

When faced with these difficulties it can be hard for everyone to remain positive – but no matter how badly things seem to be going, it is simply not acceptable for the coach to become agitated and grumpy. Rowers do not enjoy rowing when the boat is not running properly, or is constantly dipping before the catch, and they will do everything they can to improve the situation.

I remember one very sobering comment made to me by an athlete: he said that I sometimes made him and his crew members feel that they were rowing badly, just to annoy me! I sincerely hope I no longer make athletes feel like this.

Putting on a Brave Face

It can of course be extremely difficult not to become irritable and annoyed when things are not going as well as hoped, but as a coach you have a duty to your athletes to try.

The overriding consideration for the coach should be to do what is in the best interests of the team. As I mentioned earlier, the crew will scrutinize your every word, every facial expression, 'throw-away comment' and general demeanour, for signs that you too are feeling as desperate as they are. And if they sense that

you are, they will feel justified in being depressed – but if what they see is a coach explaining that whilst everything is far from rosy, **neither is it hopeless**, they will respond positively.

Helping Rowers Remain Focused

Part of the job of the coach is to help athletes remain focused on whatever aspect of their performance they are trying to improve. It is all very well for coaches to programme in hours and hours of steady state rowing, but we must remember that it is not easy for rowers to concentrate on a particular point for long periods of time. Although by its very nature rowing is extremely repetitive, successful coaches must find ways to help their rowers concentrate fully on the task at hand.

One of the ways you can achieve this is by breaking down the workload into manageable chunks, with a different focus for each one. In

The 1996 Danish lightweight men's quadruple scull showing excellent focus and concentration on the task at hand.

the case of oxygen utilization training for example, it is possible to take a one-hour session and break it down into five-minute segments. This means that for five minutes the rowers would concentrate on one aspect of technique, perhaps the speed of the hands lifting at the catch. For the next five minutes they could focus on the speed of the leg drive, before returning to focus on the hand speed. I have found this to be a very effective technique in helping to alleviate boredom and in maximizing the improvements gained throughout a training session.

This technique can of course be used effectively for much shorter work pieces. Three-minute pieces can be broken down into three one-minute chunks, where each minute has a different technical focus. During the first minute, the emphasis may be on establishing the correct rhythm and rate. The second minute could focus on the quickness of the catches, whilst the final minute focuses on having a strong, accelerated finish. The workload is more manageable when broken down in this way, and from the athlete's perspective the time seems to pass more quickly!

OPPORTUNITIES FOR IMPROVEMENT

In considering the repetitive nature of rowing, I am reminded of one of the reasons I enjoy the sport so much: it is that during the course of a training session or race, the rower has so many opportunities to improve – every single stroke represents an opportunity to improve on your previous best. Even during a race situation it is possible to improve stroke by stroke. Contrast this with many other sports, where the athlete operates in a less controlled environment; the tennis player for instance, who has to respond to his opponent's shot – he never knows what is going to come next, what

stroke he will have to play. If you can get across to your rowers this idea of having countless opportunities to improve, they will almost certainly progress more quickly.

Allowing Time for Improvements to Happen

When working on a particular aspect of technique it is essential that we allow sufficient time for adaptation to take place. As most coaches (and rowers) know, the longer you have been doing something in a certain way the longer it will take to change it. If a rower has been leaning away from his rigger for five years, he is not going to be able to stop doing so in five, ten or fifteen sessions. It is essential therefore, to be realistic about the changes in technique possible for a given time period, such as a racing season. When a particular movement pattern becomes habitual, we talk about it becoming 'grooved in'. Many studies have shown that in order for something to become a habit it needs to have been repeated a minimum of thirty times.

From my own experience this is true. I spent many years working in private health clubs and so was able to experience at first hand how difficult it could be for members to incorporate regular exercise into their lives. For most health clubs, attracting members to join is not a problem: the problem is keeping them. The attrition rate in the first three months is very high. One rule of thumb by which we operated, was that if we could help and encourage a member to attend the gym three times a week for three months, we had a very good chance of keeping him as a member. What we were trying to do, of course, was help him develop the *habit* of exercising.

In rowing it is exactly the same: we are trying to encourage our rowers to develop the habit of rowing subconsciously in a particular manner. In fact what we are trying to do is to replace one habit with another. If you have ever tried to diet or to stop smoking for example, you will appreciate how difficult it can be to break a habit.

Checking Understanding

You need to check the rowers' understanding of what it is you are asking them to do; needless to say, if they do not understand, or do not agree with what you are saying, progress will be very slow.

One way of doing this is to ask them a great many questions. You should always ask them how they feel they are rowing, before making your own observations. And when you have asked them to make a change to their technique, ask them if it feels different or better. If it does, ask them to explain in what way, what have they done that is different?

When rowers perform a movement correctly, you need to reinforce this. I often ask them to close their eyes, to focus on the way it feels when they *are* doing it correctly – that is a gold medal feeling, and anything else is second best.

Rowers must also agree that they need to change, and you must ensure they are really convinced that what you are suggesting will make them go faster. Using a video camera is an excellent way of achieving this: showing them *what* they need to change, explaining *how* to change it, and getting them to agree, will help achieve progress more quickly.

Finally, encourage rowers to comment on other crew members whilst they are watching the video; this is an excellent way to check understanding! If they can identify in others both good points and also areas that need improvement, it shows that they understand what is being sought after.

Throwing down the Gauntlet

Finally, you should try to devise as many challenges for your rowers to overcome as possible. They need only be simple, such as rowing with square blades without touching the water for ten minutes, or improving an aspect of their technique by a certain amount, as agreed between you. You should plan for a challenge in every session; success in every session; and a variety of challenges; and remember:

Every stroke you allow your crew to row badly, is a one stroke advantage to their opposition

7 Constructing a Training Programme

The first and most obvious area that needs to be considered when constructing a training programme is its principal aim. It may be to prepare the athlete for a specific race or series of races, or to rectify a weakness in the athlete's performance, in strength or flexibility for instance. And once the overall target is established, whatever it may be, then a method of determining progress towards achieving it must also be worked out, together with intermediate goals.

In rowing, as with most sports, the intermediate targets or goals tend to be geared towards such ultimate goals as winning a medal at a particular event such as the world or national championships. Now, although these goals have their place, they are not necessarily the best ones to choose. The biggest problem is that they depend entirely on outside influences. During the course of a particular race, an athlete has no influence over what the other people in the race do, and so has no control over whether or not he reaches his desired goal. Only one thing is guaranteed: that *every* competitor in that race wants to win the gold medal, and so if there are six crews in the race, all with the target of winning gold, five crews are not going to reach it. So even if you have the best row of your life, covering the course faster than you have ever done before, you will not necessarily fulfil your objective – does this mean you have failed?

It is far better to focus on performance goals which you can directly control, whether or not you achieve them. An example of such a goal is aiming for a specific improvement in technique. Performance goals also include such things as target times for ergometer or water work. For instance, it may be that in order to achieve selection for a race you need to be able to row 2,000m on the ergometer in a specific time. Alternatively, you may need to cover 5,000m in your sculling boat in less than thirty minutes or so. If you know what your overall goal is, it makes it much easier to plan your training programme.

As discussed in Chapter 8, regular evaluation of your progress towards your goals is vital in helping you to remain motivated, particularly during the long winter months. Without specific targets to work towards, it can seem as though you are just training for the sake of training, and very few people find training for its own sake rewarding: they need a sense of purpose to make it worthwhile.

GETTING STARTED

Having decided your overall target focusing on performance goals you then need to assess how close to achieving these goals you are, and what you need to do to meet them.

It may be that, in order to improve your time for 2,000m you need to become stronger in the upper body, or to improve your aerobic fitness. Whatever areas you need to improve upon, **it is important to identify them right at the very start of the planning process.**

There is no point in attempting to improve everything, if you only need to improve on one or two key areas. The essential thing is to focus closely on specific areas depending on your needs.

Deciding the Intermediate Goals

The next step is therefore to draw up some intermediate goals. If we use the example of strength training, your overall target may be to improve your maximum bench pull by 30 per cent. Thus if you can currently lift 100kg, your target will be to lift 130kg. Your intermediate goals therefore may be to lift 110kg after two months, 115kg after three months and so on until you reach 130kg. Remember that it is important to be realistic about how quickly you can hope to improve your performance.

When it comes to rowing, there are many variables which contribute to moving the boat quickly, including strength, flexibility, aerobic and anaerobic fitness, and technique. Improving just one aspect will not necessarily lead to a radical improvement in your time over the race distance. Nevertheless, you should identify the areas where you are weakest and plan accordingly.

TRAINING METHODS

With your intermediate goals established, you need to consider what training methods are the most appropriate to help you accomplish your aims. It is likely that you will end up with a range of training types, and it is therefore essential to prioritize them.

Monitoring Progress

One of the most important aspects of constructing a training programme is to incor-porate regular evaluation sessions to monitor how effective the programme is. This done, you can work out exactly what to do in each individual training session. Immediately following your evaluation sessions, you may need to modify the programme content depending on whether or not you are meeting your aims. The whole process can be summarized as follows:

1. Assess the areas where your performance is weak;
2. Identify your overall goal (performance rather than outcome);
3. Set intermediate goals;
4. Choose appropriate types of training;
5. Programme in evaluation sessions;
6. Decide on the specific content of the sessions;
7. Evaluate the success of the programme;
8. Modify the programme if necessary.

The above principles are a useful guide for preparing any type of training programme. However, before we look in more detail at how to put together a programme for rowing, there are three fundamental aspects that should be considered, the most crucial of these being perhaps overcompensation.

Overcompensation

Overcompensation refers to the ability of the body to adapt to a given load: simply put, it will adapt to any load or stress placed upon it, and once it has overcome a specific load, its immediate reaction is to make certain that, should it encounter that load again, it is better able to cope with it.

This ability of the body to constantly adapt to loading forms the backbone of all training, and without it we would never be able to improve our strength or our flexibility, for example. We would be forced to accept that however strong or supple we were, that would

105

be it, and we would never get any stronger or any more flexible – our performance level would be set and the only way we could improve it would be to increase our technical proficiency.

This process of adapting is closely linked to physical fatigue. We know that immediately following exercise the body goes through a period where it has a reduced capability – in other words, it becomes fatigued. It is *as it recovers* that it adapts, and the crucial difference is that not only does it adapt to overcome the same load again, but it adapts to overcome an *increased* load. (This process of adaptation is clearly illustrated in Fig. 19.) Thus by systematically overloading the body, we can raise the resistance that it can overcome; in other words, we can lift heavier weights or row faster, for longer.

The process is not quite as straightforward as it seems, however, because the body will not adapt to just any old load, it has to be a sufficiently difficult load before any adaptation will occur. In practical terms, if muscles are to adapt they need to be stressed to a high level; if the load is too easy, the body will simply not adapt in the desired manner. In a similar way, if you were to train with the same load for days on end, you would not find any adaptation beyond that gained in the initial few training sessions. It is essential therefore constantly to increase the load you train with, whilst allowing sufficient time to recover.

Failing Adaptation, or Overtraining

There is one important proviso to this process, and that is that the body must be allowed sufficient time to adapt. If it is not, you will enter a period of so called 'failing adaptation', where

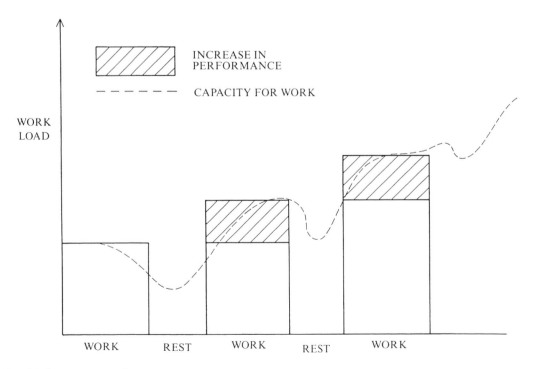

Fig. 19 Overcompensation.

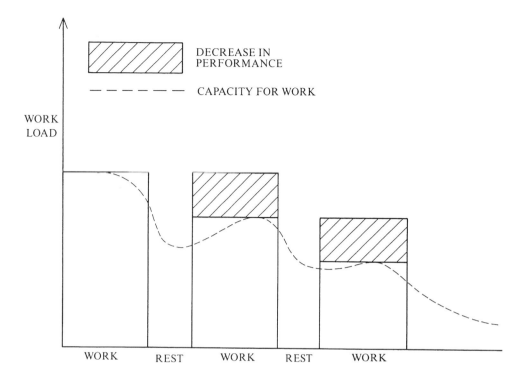

Fig. 20 Failing adaptation.

it fails to adapt to training in the desired way. Thus rather than adapting in a positive way to the stresses placed upon it, it will react in a negative way by becoming unable to overcome the load; and if this situation continues, the load that can be overcome will deteriorate until such time as the athlete is unable to train effectively.

Failing adaptation is more commonly referred to as 'overtraining', and athletes and coaches should always be aware that whilst it is common for athletes in serious training to carry with them a certain amount of residual fatigue, it is crucial that this is kept within manageable proportions. Athletes can become overtrained in two ways: simply by doing too much training, or through not allowing sufficient time for recovery. As outlined earlier, the adaptations brought about by training do not occur whilst actually exercising, but during the rest period immediately following the exercise. If you do not allow enough time to recover between training sessions, you will effectively start each subsequent session with a progressively higher level of fatigue, rather than the ability to overcome a greater load.

Current thinking on overtraining is to acknowledge that whilst training is certainly a contributing factor, it is not the only one. Athletes, like most people, are faced with a variety of different stresses in their everyday life, which may include exam or work pressures, financial problems, or relationship difficulties. The main difficulty that many face, is the day-to-day hassle of fitting the need to train into existing work commitments. Some stresses, such as exams, come and go; others are constantly in the background. When looked at in this way, it is clear that the term 'overtraining' is inadequate, and it is therefore becoming more common to use the phrase 'overstress'.

Periodization

Periodization refers to the way in which training types are alternated throughout the year. It is not possible to train everything at maximum effort at the same time. For example, if you were training every day to improve your maximum strength, you would find it very difficult, if not impossible, to do miles of high intensity rowing each day as well. To resolve this problem we therefore place a greater emphasis on particular types of training, in turn, at different times of the year, whilst at the same time trying to maintain the progress achieved in the other areas.

Although periodization is a relatively straightforward concept, it is an area that can lead to confusion because it is too easy to make it more complicated than it really is. We know that the main elements that rowers need to train are:

- Maximum strength
- Strength endurance
- Power
- Flexibility/mobility
- Aerobic capacity
- Anaerobic capacity

If you accept that you cannot hope to improve all of these at the same time, it is clear you need to devise some sort of prioritized structure. The usual way to do this is to work back from the most important race of the year and decide on how best to fit in all of the elements.

Peaking for the Overall Goal

The final area you must consider when drawing up your programme is 'peaking', and of all the areas involved in preparing for a race, it is one of the least understood. In fact peaking is simply a planning process designed to ensure that you are able to give your best performance during a specific event.

To perform at your best you need to be capable of giving your absolute maximum from both a physiological and a psychological point of view, and to achieve this you need to be totally rested mentally and physically. If you are suffering from any fatigue at all, you will not be able to perform at your maximum ability. Peaking aims therefore to remove the possibility of fatigue affecting your performance. So how do you set about peaking for the big race?

First, peaking is not something that you should leave until the last moment. Although the last few weeks before the event are critical, if you want to ensure that you give your maximum performance *on the day*, you need to start planning for it right at the start of your training, that is when you begin winter training. **Peaking is essentially the end product of the periodization of your training.**

We have discussed prioritizing training types; the next step is to build in a system of alternating the training load. You should aim to increase the workload through the season gradually, alternating between low, medium, high and maximum loadings as you go along; this is indicated in Fig. 21. This constant alternation between the differing loads will stimulate the body to adapt and will hopefully increase your *potential* performance. What will also happen is that you will build up a certain amount of residual fatigue.

Residual fatigue is experienced by all athletes. It is that constant feeling of tiredness

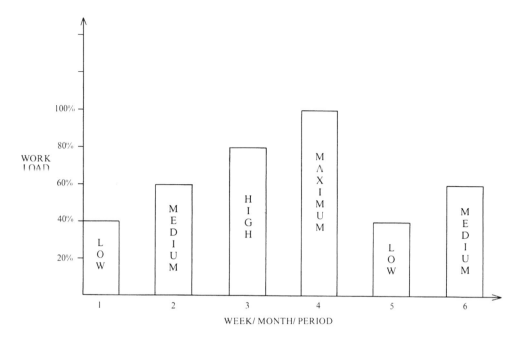

Fig. 21 Variation in training load throughout the year.

you have, that is always in the background; it should not be so large that it impinges on your training, but it will actually prevent you from performing at your absolute best. As you get nearer to your big race so you will need to remove your residual fatigue if you are to perform at your maximum potential; this means reducing your workload in the final weeks before the race. In short, the peaking process should ensure that you remove all, or most of your residual fatigue. So how do you go about achieving this? During the final seven to ten days before your main race, the *quality* of your training should be increased, with a subsequent reduction in the total quantity of work. You should concentrate on **maximum effort for shorter duration pieces**, whilst maintaining aerobic fitness.

There is no magic formula for ensuring that all residual fatigue is removed, or that you will be at your absolute peak for your big race. In my experience, however, most crews **do not wind down their training enough in the final few weeks**. It can be difficult to know what the optimum reduction in training is, but a good rule of thumb is to cut down the volume of your training by a minimum of 30 per cent – some crews cut down by anything up to 50–60 per cent with no ill effects. Never forget that whilst you need to cover miles and miles of rowing in order to *develop* your aerobic fitness, you do not need to do so to *maintain* it.

Another rule of thumb often used is that the total time spent on maximum (flat out) work for any individual session during the final seven to ten days should not exceed the time required to cover the race distance. In other words, if the race will take you seven minutes, you should not do more than seven minutes maximum work during any one training session.

109

It should be remembered that these are only guidelines and should be treated as such. They provide a good starting point, but are no substitute for experimenting with different workloads and carefully monitoring the results.

THE ROWING YEAR

In practice the rowing year is divided into three main phases, each of which is designed to enhance a particular aspect of training. They are known as the transition, preparation and competition phases.

The preparation and competition phases are each broken down into two subdivisions: the former into periods concentrating on first general, then on specific fitness; the latter into the pre-competition and the competition periods. If this all sounds a bit confusing, take a look at the table below which may help to make things clearer.

Phase	Month	Aims
Transition	September	Mental and physical recuperation
Preparation		
General	Oct–Nov	General endurance
	Dec–Jan	Maximum strength
Specific	Feb–Mar	Power
		Strength endurance
Competition		
Pre-competition	Apr–May	Strength retention and boat speed
Competition	Jun–Aug	Strength retention and boat speed

Fig. 22 Main periods of the rowing year.

Transition Period

The transition phase normally lasts for four weeks, in September, and is when athletes have the chance to recuperate from the rigours of the racing season. It should represent the ideal opportunity to get away from the constant physical stress of training. Nor should the psychological impact of training be underestimated, and mental recuperation is every bit as important as the physiological; this is particularly true for rowers who have been training at a high level for many years. Moreover, if you never have a break from training, it can be extremely difficult to remain fully motivated towards achieving your goals.

During this phase you should try to take a complete break from rowing. If this doesn't appeal, you could try doing something within rowing that presents a different challenge. For instance, if you normally row in a crew boat, you could try single sculling; alternatively, if you normally train in a single scull, why not try a coxless pair? What is important is that you have a break from the combination you have been rowing in for the previous eleven months. This does not mean that you should stop training altogether: it is better to enjoy some form of physical activity such as playing other sports, swimming or cycling for example.

Preparation Period

The principle aim of this period is to prepare yourself for competition, and it is probably the most important period of the year for any athlete. If you cut corners at this time you will almost certainly face the consequences come the regatta season, because without a sound preparation you cannot hope to achieve any real degree of success.

The work you will do during this period is largely governed by what your ultimate goals are. The higher the goal, the more work you need to put in: there are no shortcuts in the pursuit of excellence. One thing is for certain, that for every mile you row and for every weight-training session you do, there will always be someone else who has done more. Whenever I see athletes begin to take the preparation period for granted, I think of one of my first coach's favourite sayings:

> The will to win is one thing. The will to prepare to win is another.

He always said that he would rather coach rowers with the latter attribute, and I have certainly found this to be true, for if you have not done the work beforehand, you can have as much determination as you like, but you will still not win the race.

One of the challenges that we face in rowing at the moment is that to be even moderately successful in terms of winning races, you need to do a lot of training. It never ceases to amaze me how unrealistic many rowers appear to be. They expect to have a chance of winning Henley, but are only prepared to train for perhaps two water sessions at the weekend and maybe two nights through the week. Unfortunately those days are probably gone for good.

The preparation period is divided into two main phases, as we have seen, concentrating on general fitness, then on specific aspects of fitness training.

October–November

The first phase is largely devoted to improving all-round fitness. Training will focus initially on restoring previous levels of strength, and the aerobic fitness that may have been lost between the end of the racing season and the beginning of winter training. It should provide the opportunity to ease back into training after your break.

This stage should not be rushed, because it will take time for your body to become accustomed to training again. It goes without saying that the longer you have been away from training, or the less you have done during the interim period, the longer it will take to regain full fitness. You should therefore avoid the temptation to resume immediately the level at which you were training before your break. I am sure you are all familiar with the aches and pains of getting back into shape again, particularly with weight training.

There are probably more injuries caused at this time of year than at any other stage of the season. To help avoid this, it is essential to plan the initial four weeks of training with great care, and to set yourself realistic targets. If you have lost some strength, as you almost certainly will have, you need to allow yourself some time to be able to lift the same weight as you could previously. This will not happen within a few sessions, it will probably take at least four weeks. The same will be true for circuit training: having done relatively little for anything up to two months, you are asking for trouble if you go straight into full-blown circuit training.

Flexibility, too, will have deteriorated if you have not done any regular stretching during your break. Particular care should therefore be taken to restore previous levels of flexibility if you are to avoid the risk of injuries such as torn ligaments or strained muscles.

December–January

This is also a period for restoring previous fitness levels, although the emphasis on land begins to move away from general endurance and strength, towards developing maximum strength. With only eight weeks devoted to this area of training, time spent planning

111

beforehand is well spent. For instance, in a typical training programme there may be just three maximum strength training sessions per week; multiplied by the number of weeks, you can see there are usually only about twenty-four sessions set aside for this area of training – so plan very carefully if you want to get the most out of this period.

February–March

This period concentrates on specific areas of fitness. Having improved your maximum strength, you now need time to develop the fast, explosive power essential in rowing. As outlined in Chapter 5, maximum power can only be developed by improving maximum strength, which is why you should train for maximum strength first, and *then* train for power. During this period the focus also changes towards developing strength endurance.

The Competition Period

As you approach the competition period, so the focus changes more to the precise require-ments of racing; this implies a greater focus on developing boat speed. This is helped by the fact that it starts to become lighter in the evenings, enabling you to spend more time training in the boat.

April–May

At this time of year it can be all too easy to undo some of the progress you have made during the preparation period. It is essential, therefore, that you **continue to do some strength training**; this should take the form of strength retention work, ideally performed at least twice per week. You will find that if you only do it once a week, you will be very stiff the following day, and this will have an adverse effect on your other training.

As regards work on the water, the bulk of it will still be aerobic, although some sessions will be dedicated to higher intensity work. This type of training is necessary, not just for improving the anaerobic system, but also in helping to raise the rating to the required level for racing.

The question of how best to get the rating up to racing rate has in my view become more important with the change in overall training emphasis that has occurred in recent years. Whereas we used to spend anything up to 50 per cent of our training doing shorter, higher rate work, we now spend most of our training time rating no more than twenty-four strokes per minute. This has made it essential to plan just how you are going to get the rate up to the thirty-six to forty strokes per minute needed for racing. This subject is discussed in more detail a little later, in the section on progressing your programme.

April and May should be the hardest months in terms of overall levels of training. There will probably not be a large variation in your workload from one week to the next as you try to maximize the time you have before the start of the racing season proper.

June–August

For the majority of club rowers, the main regattas of the year will fall between June and the middle of July/August. The greatest change to your training at this time will be the need to alternate your workload to accommo-date racing. You should be following a pattern of cyclic loading, where you build up the intensity of your training, followed by a short period of unloading – *ie* reduced workload – immediately before a regatta.

As in April and May, the bulk of your training should still be long distance rowing at low to medium intensity. Probably the single biggest mistake that many crews – or coaches – make is to neglect this type of training during the summer months. Just as with strength training, you need to work to maintain the improvements in your aerobic fitness, as they are all too easily lost.

Although it is important to do anaerobic work, there is no need to dedicate endless sessions to it. If you have done the aerobic work through the winter, it should be relatively straightforward to improve your anaerobic capacity. Unlike the aerobic system, the anaerobic system can be trained quite quickly and so does not need vast amounts of time dedicated to it. Specific training sessions can be used to enhance this aspect of your performance, but don't go overboard; one or two sessions a week will be more than adequate.

Always remember that the **competition period is a time for perfecting technique at racing speed**.

PUTTING YOUR PROGRAMME TOGETHER

We must now consider how best to incorporate the different types of training required for success into the training programme. Although you should prioritize those aspects of your performance that are weakest, there are some general guidelines that apply to everyone. Moreover, as rowing is predominantly an aerobic event, the bulk of your training should focus on improving your aerobic capacity.

Whilst there are no hard and fast rules about the exact percentage of time you should devote to each training type, the table below will give you a good indication of the sort of split currently advocated by the ARA – and for those of you who have already worked out that the figures for each period do not total 100 per cent, the remaining time is dedicated to strength, flexibility and regeneration training.

Time of year	UT2	UT1	AT	TR	L	AL
Preparation	56	5.5	1	2	0	0
Competition	39	22.5	2.5	7.5	1.5	0.5

Fig. 23 ARA recommendations for training (per cent).

There are a few points in the table to which I would like to draw your attention. First is the amount of time spent on UT training: during the preparation period, just over 60 per cent of your training should be UT work, and this is maintained throughout the competition period with the emphasis shifting towards UT1, rather than UT2 training. **This means that the bulk of your training will be low intensity, long duration rowing at a low rate.**

The other main point, which follows on from the first, is how little time is spent on lactate training – less than 2 per cent even during the competition period.

I have to say at this stage, that whilst I agree with the principles contained in the table, I know that in reality many crews will race in various head-of-the-river races. If you hope to do well in these – and in particular the main head races – you will need to include some speed work, including lactate training, in your programme. This is not a problem, however, provided that the overall bias of the programme is still towards aerobic training, that is, UT, TR and AT training.

The final point to consider is that as you approach the competition period, the amount of TR training almost quadruples, while the amount of AT training reduces slightly.

In summary, then, the main points are as follows:

- approximately 60 per cent of your programme should be oxygen utilization training.

- Less than 2 per cent should be lactate training, and this should be carried out during the competition period.

- The competition period should have approximately four times more oxygen transport and oxygen utilization one training (UT1) than the preparation period.

With this information you can begin to outline the skeleton of your training programme. The following steps will help you get started:

- Decide what, and when, your main goal is.
- Working back from this, divide the programme into the three main phases: transition (one month), preparation (six months) and competition (five months).
- Subdivide these into one-month cycles.
- Determine the load for each monthly cycle: working back from the main event, divide it into low, maximum, high and medium loads.
- Decide on the intermediate goals (regattas).
- Programme in testing sessions (usually at the end of a light week).
- Decide on your overall aims for each monthly cycle.
- Determine the content of each individual session for the initial month.
- Review each month, and adapt as necessary.

PROGRESSING YOUR PROGRAMME

When you have worked out the content of your first week's training, you will need to decide how best to progress it; to do this you will need to assess the workload for each training session. This is determined by three things: the quality and the quantity of work, and the rest period.

Training load = Quality + Quantity + Rest

Fig. 24 Training load.

Assessing the Workload

When we talk about the 'quality of work' we are referring to how hard it is; it is usually expressed as the pace it is performed at, *eg* 500m split time on the ergometer, or rowing at full pressure. In the case of weight training it would be the actual weight lifted or the percentage of maximum that you work at.

Quantity refers to how many repetitions or sets are performed, *eg* three sets of twelve repetitions, six 500m pieces, or sixty minutes oxygen utilization work.

Rest is the total rest between work pieces. In the boat this may be the rest between both repetitions and sets. You may be doing two sets of three two-minute pieces ($2 \times [3 \times 2']$), with one minute rest between each two-minute piece, and ten minutes rest between each set; the total rest would therefore be fourteen minutes.

If you want to progress your programme you will need to alter one or more of these variables, by either increasing the quality, or increasing the quantity, or reducing the rest period. There are some general rules, however, that should be observed: first, it is better to change just one variable at a time because it is then far easier to monitor the effect of the change. If, for example, you increased both the quality and the quantity from one session to the next, you would not know which had had the greater effect, should you become excessively fatigued.

The other point worth mentioning is that you cannot do high levels of quality work if you are also trying to do a high quantity of work. As the level of quality increases, so the quantity needs to reduce; similarly, if you wish to do a high quantity of work, it needs to be done at a low quality. In general, it is also better to progress from quantity to quality of work because this gives your body the best chance of adapting to the workload and helps minimize the risk of injury. The annual training programme should follow this pattern.

At the beginning of winter training you should be doing lots of low intensity rowing – that is, high quantity, low quality. As you approach the competition period, so the emphasis should move towards doing more shorter periods of high intensity training – low quantity, high quality.

When it comes to rest you need to be more careful than when you alter the quantity or quality of work, because depending on the aim of the training session, you may affect the physiological adaptation that occurs by increasing or decreasing the rest period. As an example, if you were to increase the rest period between work pieces when doing lactate tolerance training, you would minimize the total amount of lactic acid produced during the session and this would lessen the training effect.

On the other hand, you cannot reduce the rest period by too much without running the risk of excessive overloading leading to chronic fatigue. Nevertheless, the rest period can be manipulated a certain amount to alter the training load: when you are doing circuit training for instance, you can reduce the rest period between exercises quite easily without doing any real harm. Similarly, you can reduce

the rest between work pieces on the water or ergometer by a small amount, so long as it remains within the guidelines specified.

Monitoring your Workload

It is essential to monitor your total workload each month and to use this information to set targets for future months. There are several ways of doing this.

One way is to record the total amount of time spent doing each type of training, for instance, the total number of minutes spent on UT2 training. This is simple to do and does not take up much time. Having gathered this information you can use the table in Fig. 23 to ensure that the balance of your programme is appropriate.

As the quantity of work should be increased throughout the preparation period, it is straightforward enough to use this sort of information to set targets for each week. If, for example, at the start of winter training you are doing a total of 200 minutes UT2 training a week, you may decide that you would like to increase this by 25 per cent over a four-week period. In this example your target would be 250 minutes in week four, 225 minutes for week two, and so on.

It is particularly easy to measure workload when doing weight training: all you need to do is use the following calculation:

(no of sets) × (no of repetitions) × (weight lifted)

This should be done for each exercise and then the total for each added together. For example, the workload for the circuit shown below would be 9,900kg, as follows:

Power clean	100kg × 3 × 12	= 3,600kg
Bench press	50kg × 3 × 12	= 1,800kg
Squat	125kg × 3 × 12	= 4,500kg
	Total	**9,900kg**

As with the previous example, this information may be used to set targets for future weeks.

Other ways to monitor training and set targets are to count the total number of minutes spent at a given rating or heart-rate zone. The former is a useful way of ensuring that you achieve a smooth transition from the relatively low rates used in winter training to the rates required for racing.

FINAL ADVICE ON WRITING A PROGRAMME

Perhaps the biggest mistake that many people make is paying too much attention to the details of preparing a training programme.

Writing a programme is relatively straightforward, as long as you let it be straightforward.

You should keep it as simple as possible. Work out the overall loads that you want for each week or month as described, and find the easiest way of accomplishing them. Programmes do not have to be filled with complicated combinations of training to be effective – remember, 60 per cent of your training is what used to be called 'steady state' rowing, and that leaves only 40 per cent for the rest.

When you have worked out how many training sessions you have per week, it is a simple matter to calculate the number of sessions that should be devoted to each type of training, using the figures given in Fig. 23.

8 Monitoring and Evaluating Progress

One of the most important aspects of any training programme is monitoring the progress made. Unfortunately it is also one of the least valued and so is often a secondary consideration when it comes to putting the programme together.

THE BENEFITS OF MONITORING TRAINING

Monitoring your progress is essential if you are to make the most of the time you dedicate to your training. There are many benefits to be gained from including regular evaluation sessions into your training programme. Monitoring your training through regular testing can:

- Identify strengths and weaknesses;
- Evaluate if your programme is having the desired effect;
- Allow you to make adjustments to your programme;
- Help you to remain motivated;
- Identify when you may be at risk from overstress;
- Predict performance potential;
- Provide information for crew selection.

Identifying Strengths and Weaknesses

At the outset of training it is important to know your various strengths and weaknesses, because without this information it is impos-

sible to know what type of training you should focus on. As everyone has a limited amount of time available for training, it is essential to use that time in the most effective way.

Evaluating the Workload

Having identified what you are going to work on, you need to know whether or not you are making progress: how will you assess this if you do not test for any improvement?

If your training programme is not having the desired effect, it is much better to find this out sooner, rather than later; with this information, you can make appropriate changes. The other thing to bear in mind is that as your body adapts to the training load, you will need to increase the load if you want to continue improving. Regular testing is one of the most effective ways of finding out when it is time to do so, and by how much.

The Effect on Motivation

In my view, the most beneficial aspect of regular testing is the effect it has on motivation. It can be very difficult to remain motivated towards training, especially during the winter months when the excitement of racing is still a long way off, and this is particularly true if you (or your athletes) have been training for many years.

By the time you have been rowing for ten years or more, the improvements you can expect to see may be very small, and when this happens it can be difficult to keep putting yourself through the grind of daily training. If, however, you can see even the smallest improvement in your performance, it is much easier to find the willpower to continue. Nobody is perfect in every sense and so there is always room for improvement – the trick is finding the best way of showing it.

Recognizing Overstress

The demands being placed nowadays on competitive rowers have never been so great and the possibility of becoming overtrained is more likely than at any stage in the past. It is also generally agreed that the term 'over-trained' is in itself misleading.

Athletes have many stresses to cope with in the course of their day-to-day life – training is only one of them. Thus, when an athlete shows signs of overtraining, it may not necessarily have been brought on by his training alone; he may have additional stresses to cope with at work, or be studying for important exams, or be having difficulties in his closest relationship for example. These additional stress factors will contribute to the psychological load he must overcome every day. A more accurate description of overtraining is therefore **overstress**.

There is a great deal of research being conducted at the moment into overstress syndrome: the main problem is that it is very difficult to predict when an athlete is about to become overstressed. Researchers are therefore trying to find a test that will assess exactly that – and in the meantime, the best guide is knowing yourself (or your rowers) and being 'in tune' with what your body is telling you.

If you can recognize when your body is saying 'enough' and take a break from your training, you will be some way towards being able to deal with the situation.

Predicting Performance Potential

Although it may not be particularly relevant for most clubs or rowers, testing can be used to predict an athlete's potential performance. At international level, many countries use testing to 'stream' their athletes, focusing resources on those that have the 'right' physiological attributes for top class performance.

The difficulty is, that although there are some distinctive physiological characteristics that are advantageous for international level rowers, there are always exceptions to the rule, athletes who make it to the very top despite having relatively 'inferior' physiology.

A Guide to Crew Selection

Test results are undoubtedly an invaluable tool for coaches when it comes to selecting crews, providing they are used wisely – although they are *not* a substitute for knowing your rowers. They can be most helpful in situations where it is all but impossible to separate rowers technically. For example, if you have whittled a squad down to the final nine rowers for an eight, and cannot distinguish between two of them for the final place, how do you decide?

You have one of two options: you can make a subjective decision based on your 'gut' feeling; or you can use the results of an ergometer test. Most athletes would prefer the final decision to be based on some form of quantifiable data, rather than one which is purely subjective.

GUIDELINES FOR TESTING

Whatever type of testing you decide to do there are some simple rules that should be applied. Any test used must be:

- Relevant
- Valid
- Reproducible
- Sports specific
- Standardized

Relevant

It is important to ensure that the tests you choose are relevant. Although this may seem obvious, there are many tests available that are *not* particularly relevant for rowers. One example is the 'one rep maximum lift' test used in weight lifting: as power is more important to rowers than absolute strength, there is no real benefit in finding out how much weight you can lift on just one occasion for a given exercise. Testing over three repetitions, however, will give you sufficient information for exercise prescription and monitoring progress.

Valid

A test is valid depending on whether it measures what it aims to. A good example of this is the 'sit and reach' test, often used to measure flexibility of the hamstrings, but one which in fact is better for measuring lower back flexibility. If you have an inflexible lower back, it is this that will prohibit you reaching forwards rather than your hamstrings.

Another example of a test that is not necessarily valid is the sit-up test to indicate abdominal strength. In fact the hip flexors are used more during sit-ups than the abdominal muscles, making the sit-up test invalid as an indicator of abdominal strength.

Reproducible

You must be able to replicate the test for it to be of any practical use: if you are unable to replicate it, how will you know whether you

have improved in any way? For a test to be reproducible, you must also be able to get the same result if it is repeated very soon afterwards; and if you get a range of different results, it is very difficult to know with any certainty whether the results are valid.

Sports specific

Perhaps the most obvious rule is that, where possible, a test should be sports specific. It is well known that runners get different results when tested on a treadmill as compared with being tested on a cycle. Similarly, rowers will produce different results when tested on a treadmill as compared with a rowing ergometer. All movements carried out during the test should therefore simulate the rowing action as closely as possible.

Standardized

One area to which you should pay particular attention is the standardizing of the way tests are carried out. The more areas you can standardize when testing, the more reliable your results will be. If you do a warm-up beforehand for instance, try to do the same warm-up every time; if you plan on doing a battery of tests in a session, make sure that you always do them in the same order. And if you are going to use an ergometer, always use the same one; do not assume that you will get the same results from each machine, because you will not!

One area of particular importance is measuring the heart rate, which is probably more variable than any other physiological parameter you are likely to measure. It varies from week to week, day to day, even hour to hour, so if you keep a record of your own heart rate, always measure it at the same time of day.

TYPES OF LAND TEST

There are many different categories of test that you can choose from, but the three most common are anthropometric, physiological and psychological tests.

Anthropometric Tests

These tests measure height, arm span, shoulder width, leg length and trunk height, and although, strictly speaking, weight is not an anthropometric test, it is usually included in this category. They are of most benefit to those coaching juniors who are still growing, because if you measure their various parameters regularly, it is a good way of assessing their stage of development.

This information can be invaluable in helping to explain why some of your rowers suddenly start to struggle with their training. It may be that they are experiencing a spurt in growth – it is known, for instance, that boys peak in growth rate for both height and weight around the age of fourteen, reaching their final height by the time they are seventeen or eighteen. Girls develop much earlier, having their peak *height* spurt at about twelve years and their weight spurt approximately six months later. The other major difference between the sexes in this respect is that girls reach their final height earlier than boys, typically at about fifteen years.

Growing uses a lot of energy, and if a rower is developing rapidly it can be very difficult for him to cope with the demands of the training programme; you may, as a result, have to review it. And if children are still growing there is an increased likelihood of injury, particularly to their epiphyseal plates (growth plates) should they lift heavy loads. Only when children have stopped growing is it safe for them to commence heavy weight training.

Taking these measurements regularly may also help to explain rigging problems. A coach once sought my advice on what he could do about the technique of one of his junior boys, who was having great difficulty with his finishes. In fact we had adjusted his foot stretcher to what was the correct position less than three weeks previously, so I went out in the coaching launch, made sure that he was adjusted 'properly', and then observed his sculling.

It was obvious straightaway that his foot stretcher was positioned too near the bow of the boat. This meant that his finish position was too far towards the bow, allowing his hands to come past his body. As it happened, he was due to come into the laboratory that evening for testing, and so we duly measured, among other things, his height – and discovered he had grown by over half a centimetre!

The relationship between leg length and trunk height can also alter the effect of rigging. If, for example, one of your rowers has grown by two centimetres or so, their legs may remain the same length, but their trunk height will have increased, and this will have an effect on which muscles are utilized during the draw part of the stroke. This is of particular significance in sculling where you should be aiming to draw the oar handle through at a relatively high position.

Physiological Tests

Physiological tests fall into seven specific areas: maximum strength, strength endurance, power, aerobic capacity, anaerobic capacity, flexibility and speed. With the possible exception of speed, rowing programmes should include tests for all of these.

Within the limited space of this book it is not possible to give an exhaustive evaluation of all the tests that are available. I have therefore tried to explain the procedures of those that are most commonly used. You should

120

bear in mind, however, that if you cannot do a particular test for any reason, perhaps through lack of equipment, there may be others that you could do instead.

The number one rule for testing is that it must be carried out on a regular basis. Doing a test once will not give you much information, and as a general guide, I would suggest that you incorporate testing sessions into your programme approximately every four to six weeks. You don't need to do tests for all areas in the one training session – you wouldn't want to test for aerobic capacity on the same night as doing a maximum strength test, for example. By staggering the tests over a series of sessions, it is far easier to incorporate them into your programme. Besides, as discussed in Chapter 5, your training programme will emphasize certain types of training at different times of the year, and this will determine what tests you should carry out at that time; thus if you are training for maximum strength, you should test for maximum strength.

There are, of course, some tests that can be done throughout the year, such as flexibility and anaerobic threshold.

The schedule of tests I would recommend you do is shown in the accompanying table, and we will now look at them in more detail.

Characteristic	Type of Test	Equipment
Maximum Strength	3 rep maximum	Weights
Maximum power	10 strokes	Ergometer
Strength endurance	Bench pull	Weights
Aerobic capacity	2,000/5,000m	Ergometer
Anaerobic capacity	30 seconds	Ergometer
Anaerobic Threshold	Incremental	Ergometer: Heart rate monitor
Flexibility	Hamstring	Floor mat

Fig. 25 Recommended test battery.

Maximum Strength

Testing for maximum strength is a relatively straightforward procedure. The easiest way is gradually to increase the weight on the bar for a particular lift, for example, power clean. When you reach a weight that you cannot lift for three consecutive repetitions, this should be recorded as your maximum. There is, however, one important proviso: **the lifts should be executed with good technique**.

It is absolutely essential that good technique is maintained throughout the tests, particularly with lifts such as the power clean. Failure to do so will result in excessive training loads being recommended, but this will only encourage bad technique in training and lead to a greater risk of injury. If, for example, an athlete uses bad technique but is able to lift more weight, you should record as his maximum the last weight he lifted using good technique.

Lifts that should be included in a test battery are the power clean, the bench pull, the bench press, the leg press and squats (the half or front squat for preference).

Strength Endurance

The test that I recommend for assessing strength endurance is the bench pull test. It is widely used by the national team and is valuable in identifying weaknesses in the upper body. As the latter is used to a greater extent during the sculling movement, this test is of particular importance to scullers, and they should place a considerable emphasis on bench pulls as a training method.

The protocol for the test is as follows:

- Select the weight required (see table);

- Adjust the bench height (see note 1, below);
- Lift the bar at a rate of 28–30 lifts per minute;
- The bar must strike the bench each time, and the arms extend fully between lifts;
- The test is completed when the rower either:
    - fails to touch the bench three times in a row, or
    - is unable to maintain the rate of lifting;
- Record the total number of repetitions.

Notes:

1. The bench should be adjusted so that whilst holding the bar with arms fully extended, the weight discs are just clear of the floor, that is, they do not touch the floor. It is a good idea to place some mats below the weights.

2. **It is important to find a weight that you can lift for approximately six to seven minutes.** If you cannot achieve this using the recommended weights, use a lighter weight.

Category	Heavyweight	Lightweight	Junior
Male	40–50kg	35–45kg	30–40kg
Female	20–25kg	20–25kg	15–25kg

Fig. 26 Guidelines for the bench pull test.

Power

One of the simplest ways of monitoring your maximum power is to do a ten-stroke test on the ergometer. All you need do is set the

The start position for the bench pull test.

The finish position for the bench pull test.

ergometer on whatever setting you prefer, perform a brief warm-up, stop, make sure the flywheel is not moving, and then do ten maximum pressure strokes.

Depending on which ergometer you use, you can then simply record the average watts over the ten strokes. It is better, however, to disregard the first few strokes in order to compensate for the fact that you need to get the flywheel moving. In this case you should record the scores for the final five strokes only.

Aerobic Capacity

There are any number of tests you can do to monitor aerobic capacity, the majority of them being done on the ergometer. Two of the most common distances are 2,000m and 5,000m. I would recommend that you do a 2,000m test at the start of your winter

training and then alternate this with a 5,000m test after four to six weeks, thus 2,000m, then a 5,000m, then a 2,000m.

If you want to assess improvements in efficiency at the same time, you can simply set a rating for the tests. Setting a standardized rating makes it very straightforward to work out power output per stroke, because all you have to do is divide the distance covered by the number of strokes taken. This can be an effective tool in ensuring that you increase

Test distance	2,000m
Time taken	8 minutes
Rating	26 strokes per minute
Total number of strokes	208 (8 × 26)
Distance covered per stroke	= $\dfrac{\text{Test distance}}{\text{number of strokes}}$
	= 2,000 divided by 208
	= 9.61m/stroke

Fig. 27 Working out the distance covered per stroke.

your power output per stroke, rather than getting a better score simply by increasing the rating. Fig. 27 shows how to work out the distance covered per stroke: power output per stroke.)

Anaerobic Capacity

As your total performance is made up of both your aerobic and your anaerobic capacities, it is important to assess both of them. The test used for measuring anaerobic capacity can be done using an ergometer. As with all tests you should do a warm-up beforehand. Set up the ergometer for a thirty-second work piece and to show watts; after warming up, perform a maximum, flat-out effort over the time, and record the average power output (watts).

Anaerobic Threshold

To get an accurate measurement of your anaerobic threshold (AT) you really do need to do an incremental test on the ergometer with someone taking blood samples at the end of each workload. Unfortunately, not everyone has access to a laboratory where this can be done; it may be that the cost involved is prohibitive, or perhaps there isn't a laboratory within a reasonable distance.

It is quite possible nevertheless to assess your AT with a heart-rate monitor and an ergometer – although I have to say that whilst the procedure is relatively straightforward, it is not foolproof. Some studies have shown that, in anything up to 50 per cent of cases it is not possible to identify with any degree of accuracy where the AT occurs using heart rate

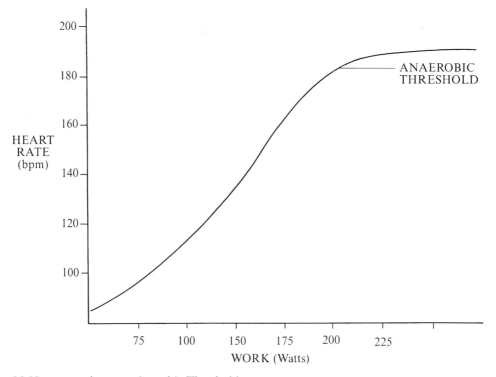

Fig. 28 Heart rate plateau at Anerobic Threshold

alone. Without going into too much detail, the problem is that heart rates can at best only predict where the AT occurs.

I have measured many rowers myself, under laboratory conditions, using the protocol described later. When my colleagues and I tried to identify the AT by looking at the heart-rate data alone, we found that, whilst it was possible in many cases, in others it was not. We also compared the heart rate predicted AT with the AT determined through blood lactic acid samples, and found that there was a good correlation. Effectively this means that, if you can identify the AT using heart rate, it is likely to be correct.

Before doing this test, it is necessary to have completed a maximum test, such as the 2,000m test outlined earlier. You should record your maximum power output from this test and use it as the basis for working out your work increments for the AT test.

To do the test itself, you should start by doing a five-minute warm-up at 50 per cent of your maximum power output (watts); this should be followed by three minutes at 65 per cent of your maximum power. Do a further four three-minute pieces, raising the workload by 5 per cent each time, *ie* 70, 75, 80 and 85 per cent. This is performed continuously, and will give a total test time of twenty minutes.

The heart rate should be recorded every thirty seconds throughout the test. When the test is finished you should take the final three heart rates for each workload and calculate the average value. This should then be plotted against the workload, *ie* power against heart rate. The AT will show as the point at which the heart rate slope begins to level off (see Fig. 28). The table below outlines the protocol used for identifying AT using heart rate.

- Record heart rate every thirty seconds.
- Average final three readings for each workload.

Maximum test = 300 watts

AT test protocol	Workload
5' at 50% max	150
3' at 65% max	195
3' at 70% max	210
3' at 75% max	225
3' at 80% max	240
3' at 85% max	255

Fig. 29 Predicted anaerobic threshold test.

- Plot against power output (watts)

Once you have identified your AT, you can use the information to set your heart-rate zones for your training. As a guide you should allow a range of approximately ten to fifteen beats per training method. If, for example, your AT occurs at a heart rate of 170bpm, you would aim to do your AT training within the range 160–170bpm. For UT1 and UT2 training, the ranges would be 145–160bpm and 130–145bpm respectively. Oxygen transport training should be done at heart rates of 170–185bpm, whilst any training done at a heart rate above 185bpm would be appropriate for lactate training. If all this sounds confusing, take a look at Fig. 30 which shows the above example in table format.

AT test heart rate	UT2	UT1	AT	TR	L
170	130–145	145–60	160–70	170–185	185+

Fig. 30 Example of heart-rate zones following AT test (bpm).

One final consideration is that heart rate is affected by many different things, including temperature, humidity, personal hydration levels and the time of day. For instance, it tends to be lower in the morning than in the evening, which means that it can be difficult to reach your desired heart rate during early morning sessions. You should therefore aim to train at the lower end of your heart-rate range for these sessions, and at the higher end for evening sessions. For this reason it is preferable to schedule any AT, TR and lactate training for evening sessions.

Flexibility

Although it is possible to measure the flexibility of most muscle groups, the most important area for rowers to assess and monitor is the flexibility of the hamstring muscles. Many athletes use the 'sit and reach' test to do this, although it is actually better suited to assessing the flexibility of the lower back. Rather, the test described below has been recommended to me by several physiotherapists, as being far more effective at measuring hamstring flexibility than the 'sit and reach' test.

To carry out this test you first need to make sure that the rower is sufficiently warmed up to minimize any risk of injury. With the rower lying on his back the tester should raise the leg, keeping it straight, until a point is reached where the rower can no longer extend the leg. Using the example of a clock face, the tester then needs to make an estimation of what time it is, as represented by the position of the leg, eg. three o'clock. You should aim to reach to the one o'clock position at least, but preferably twelve o'clock.

Having identified the flexibility of your hamstrings, it is important to stress that, should you need to improve in this area, you cannot do so simply by doing a five-minute stretch before training: it is essential to set aside time in your training programme to do developmental stretching exercises as outlined in Chapter 5.

Monitoring your Daily Heart Rate

The final physiological test I would recommend is that you monitor your heart rate on a daily basis. As you become fitter, so your resting and exercise heart rates will become lower, and by recording your heart rate first thing every morning, you will have a detailed record of improvements in your fitness. This

Hamstring flexibility test. The position shown corresponds to approximately two o'clock.

Hamstring flexibility test. The position shown corresponds to approximately one o'clock. This is the minimum position you should be able to reach for efficient rowing.

practice may also be helpful in that it can provide an early indicator of when you are overstressed, or when your body is succumbing to some viral infection whose symptoms have not yet shown; you will then be able to modify your training before any major problem occurs.

Generally speaking, should your heart rate increase by anything over ten beats or so of your normal range, you should reduce your training load until it returns to normal.

Psychological Tests

There are many excellent books on the market which deal specifically with psychological fitness, so I have outlined only one evaluation tool which I think is of particular benefit: the 'Daily Analysis of Life Demands of Athletes' (B.S. Rushall, 1981). A tool for measuring stress in élite athletes is to be found in Y. Hanin (ed.), *Stress and Anxiety in Sport* (Moscow: Physical Culture and Sport Publishers).

This test consists of a questionnaire containing thirty-four questions which aim to assess the levels of stress an athlete faces. Twenty-five of the questions relate specifically to the symptoms of stress, while the remaining nine look at the sources of stress. The questions are graded from 'worse than normal' to 'normal' to 'better than normal'. The test only takes a few moments to complete.

By completing the questionnaire on a daily basis, a picture is built up of the athlete's 'normal' response to the various stresses encountered. If the response begins to move out of the usual (normal) range, adaptations can be made to the training programme to allow for this. This makes it a useful test for detecting signs of overstress (overtraining), and for gauging the athlete's response to new situations, for example, when travelling, at training camps, to new training schedules and so on.

To get the most from the test you need to

be 'in tune' with your body – in other words, you must be able to identify what feels normal. Although some coaches have suggested that this limits its usefulness to experienced athletes, I have used it to help less experienced rowers learn how to recognize the 'warning signs' in their bodies when they have been doing too much. I would therefore still recommend it as of help to younger athletes in developing their own body awareness.

TYPES OF WATER TEST

There are just as many tests that can be used on the water to monitor training progress, and in this section we look at how to use different assessment procedures to monitor performance, select crews and prioritize events.

Long Distance Trials

There are many ways to monitor the performance of your crew throughout the year, and during the winter months it is usual to do long distance time trials. These are normally run over a set distance which can be anywhere between 6 and 16km depending on your state of training. Ideally they should be on a straight course, with still water. Don't worry if you do not have access to this sort of water (very few people do); what matters most, is that you do the trial on a regular basis.

When it comes to the length of the course, you should if possible choose a distance that will take you more than fifteen minutes to row. This will help minimize the disruption to your training. If the course is too short, you will tend to go over at a rating which is too high for the time of year. You can, if you like, set yourself a cap for the rating just as you would on the ergometer; this will allow you to monitor your power output per stroke at the same time.

During the summer it is perfectly acceptable to continue with the long distance trials – you can simply include them as part of your training. You may also incorporate time trials over a shorter distance, for example, 1,500m. One word of caution though, should you choose to include shorter distance trials, and that is, you need to ensure that they do not conflict with your racing schedule. It is too easy to end up doing one time trial after another with regattas in between, and if you do this, you will end up with very little opportunity left for actually training.

Long distance trials can also be very useful for reducing a large squad of rowers to a smaller 'core' group. If you had a group of twenty scullers, for example, you could do a long distance time trial, identify and take out the slowest five, and then concentrate resources on the remaining fifteen.

As you get nearer the competition season, you may well face the prospect of having to identify the fastest combination of rowers for the particular events you want to race in. There are two main ways of doing this: seat racing and a pairs matrix.

Pairs Matrix

A coxless pairs matrix is used to identify a rank order for rowers on both sides of the boat, *ie* stroke side and bow side. However, because one side may be stronger than the other, a matrix should not be used to provide a rank order for the squad as a whole.

During the course of the matrix, every stroke-side rower will have the opportunity to race in a pair with every bow-side rower over a distance of 1,000 to 1,500m. Anything above this distance will lead to excessively high levels of fatigue without providing any additional significant information.

Fig. 31 illustrates a typical pairs matrix for a squad of sixteen rowers. Stroke-side rowers are numbered 1–8, whilst bow-side are coded A–H.

There are several things you need to bear in mind when using a matrix of this sort. Firstly, the matrix will favour those rowers who can adapt quickly to rowing with new partners – in the same way that those rowers who cannot adapt quickly will be at a disadvantage: this does not necessarily mean they cannot move a boat quickly, however.

The other main point is that caution must be used when forming larger boat combinations using this method. As with seat racing, having the ability to adapt to new partners and move a small boat quickly, is not the same as being able to move a large, fast boat quickly. This is particularly true in the case of selecting a quad scull by using single sculling results.

Race 1	Race 2	Race 3	Race 4	Race 5	Race 6	Race 7	Race 8
1 + B	1 + C	1 + D	1 + E	1 + F	1 + G	1 + H	1 + A
2 + C	2 + D	2 + E	2 + F	2 + G	2 + H	2 + A	2 + B
3 + D	3 + E	3 + F	3 + G	3 + H	3 + A	3 + B	3 + C
4 + E	4 + F	4 + G	4 + H	4 + A	4 + B	4 + C	4 + D
5 + F	5 + G	5 + H	5 + A	5 + B	5 + C	5 + D	5 + E
6 + G	6 + H	6 + A	6 + B	6 + C	6 + D	6 + E	6 + F
7 + H	7 + A	7 + B	7 + C	7 + D	7 + E	7 + F	7 + G
8 + A	8 + B	8 + C	8 + D	8 + E	8 + F	8 + G	8 + H

Fig. 31 Pairs matrix for sixteen rowers (taken from ARA *Silver Coaching Award Handbook*).

Seat Racing

Although a pairs matrix is useful for identifying a rank order for stroke side and bow side, seat racing is used to help find the fastest combination for a given boat. It can provide invaluable information on the compatibility of rowers within a crew.

During seat racing, a rower is swopped from one crew to another, in order to find out which combination is the quicker. If we take the example of two coxless fours, we would start off by doing one race, timing it and making any notes on conditions, steering mishaps and so on, then we could swop two rowers and repeat the race. For argument's sake, let us suppose that crew number one won the race, beating crew two by 10secs. For the second race we may decide to swop the rowers in the three seat *ie* the number three rower from crew one (A) would change places with the rower at three in crew two (B).

If crew two won this race by 10secs, we would infer that (A) was better than (B). Rower (A) would have beaten rower (B) by a total of 20secs *ie* 10secs from race one, plus 10secs from race two. Supposing, however, that crew one had won race two by 15secs, then rower (B) would have beaten rower (A) by 5secs overall *ie* 15secs minus 10secs.

One of the biggest problems with seat racing is the time it can take to find the right combination. It is therefore better to do it over several days, although this does, of course, make it difficult to ensure similar conditions for all races.

The other problem is that we are trying to find the fastest crew, *ie* the crew which will be the quickest over the race distance, during one performance. By its very nature, seat racing favours rowers who can 'survive' the process, rather than those rowers who can produce an absolute maximum performance. Seat racing

is nevertheless a valuable tool in helping to identify quick combinations of rowers.

To run seat racing successfully, you need to observe some basic rules:

- Use matched boats; coxed for preference (this eliminates steering complications).
- Do not tell the rowers in advance what the combinations for each race will be. Rowers may influence the results if they know the format!
- It is important that rowers do not know that they are being seat raced, for the same reason.
- Only change the stroke men to assess their ability to stroke the crew. Identify their ability to move the boat, using the number two seat beforehand.
- Record any steering problems, particularly shipwrecks or hitting buoys.
- Above all, do not make your decision solely on the basis of one race, especially if the time difference is minimal *eg* less than 3–4secs.

PREDICTED GOLD STANDARD TIMES

The final assessment procedure to consider is using gold standard times, and it is one of the simplest ways to determine which event you have the best chance of getting a medal in, for instance the coxless four or the coxless pair. Put simply, if you can predict what time the winning crew will do for each particular event, you can compare this with what your crew can do.

I appreciate that many crews are not composed as a result of extensive seat racing or trials; when it comes to club crews, the decision as to which event to enter is largely based on how many people are prepared to train: if there are four people they will row in a four, if there are two, they will row in a pair. Even so, for those who want to maximize their chances of winning or of getting a medal, you need to be a bit more calculating. It may be, for instance, that you would have a better chance of a medal rowing in a coxless four than in a coxed one – but how do you know, if you don't compare the likely winning times?

Standard times really come into their own where you have a large squad of rowers to choose from. It may be that you have sufficient rowers to enter an eight and a four at Henley, but are not sure which offers the best prospect for a medal.

To use standard times, you need to predict what the winning times will be for the events you are considering. You would then do a series of timed pieces, over the distance, in the different crews, for example the coxless four, the eight and so on. The final step would be to calculate the percentage gold medal time for each event; Fig. 32 shows the equation that would be used to work this out. Fig. 33 uses the example of a squad which is undecided between entering an eight or two fours, one coxed and one coxless, at the National Championships. As can be seen, the boat with the best chance of a medal is the eight, as it has a higher percentage of the predicted gold medal time when compared with the other two boats.

Predicted gold medal times can also be used when you do long distance timed pieces. The equation used is shown in Fig. 34, together with an example of the calculation.

$$\frac{\text{test distance}}{\text{race distance}} \times \frac{\text{predicted gold medal time}}{\text{test time}} \times 100 = \% \text{ gold time}$$

Fig. 34 Equation for percentage gold medal times using longer distance work pieces.

$$\frac{5,000}{2,000} \times \frac{360}{960} \times 100 = 2.5 \times 0.37 \times 100 = 92.5\%$$

eg 5,000m test piece completed in 16 minutes, with a gold medal time of 6 minutes

Fig. 35 Calculation for percentage gold medal times over longer distance work pieces (example).

USING A VIDEO TAPE RECORDER

The final and probably the most important way to monitor your progress is to record training sessions in the boat using a video camera: of all the tools available to a crew to help them improve their rowing, it is by far the most effective. Regularly recorded training sessions can provide as much feedback to a crew as can a good coach – and therein lies the nub of the situation, because very few crews use the video on a regular enough basis for it to be of any real value.

To get the most benefit from video, ideally you should try to record a session on a weekly basis; and if this is not possible, fort-

$$\frac{\text{predicted time}}{\text{actual time}} \times 100 = \text{percentage gold time}$$

Fig. 32 Calculating percentage gold time.

Boat	Time for 2000m (min)	Predicted gold medal time (min)	Test data	Percentage gold medal time (%)
8+	6.00'	5.50'	$\frac{350}{360} \times 100$	97.22
4–	6.35'	6.20'	$\frac{380}{395} \times 100$	96.20
4+	6.46'	6.28'	$\frac{388}{406} \times 100$	95.57

Fig. 33 Examples of gold medal time.

nightly, or even monthly recordings are better than nothing. Many of you probably think that getting everything organized to record just one training session, much less one session a week, is far too much trouble. You need to locate a camera, organize the launch (and driver) and make sure the batteries are charged, amongst other things, and whilst I know it can be difficult to organize all this, the benefits are just too great not to do it.

When you consider how much time and effort you put into rowing, the sacrifices you make every day of the year and the goals you set yourself, it does seem ridiculous not to make time for what is one of the most powerful aids we have to improve our rowing. I am often surprised that so many clubs do not have a video camera costing a few hundred pounds, when they have a fleet of boats worth thousands of pounds. But how can we maximize our use of the video, apart from using it regularly?

Planning What to Film

Firstly, plan what you want to film and stick to it! Avoid the temptation of trying to film the crew from every possible angle and to capture every single aspect of technique in one session. If you do this, you will simply end up with a collage of images, none of which will give you sufficient time for any real analysis; you will end up constantly using the fast forward and rewind buttons.

How Many Strokes to Film

When filming each rower you should aim to record at least ten to twenty strokes from each side of the boat. This will give the rowers enough time to process the information, without the distraction of rewinding and so on, when they come to watch the film.

Training Kit

One very simple and effective idea is to make sure that the crew comes down wearing appropriate training kit, because this can make a significant difference to the quality of the final image. Moreover, if everyone wears the same kit, it is much easier to make comparisons in body movement patterns. If they wear the usual assortment of different tops, leggings etc, it makes it more difficult to see this. Light, skin-hugging clothing works best, preferably with a stripe down the legs and arms.

Stream Conditions

When you are filming from a coaching launch, the image will be less shaky if you film when the crew is going with the stream. If the conditions are windy, filming should be done with a tail wind for the same reason.

Telephoto Lens

All video cameras have a zoom facility, but this should be used with caution because constantly zooming in and out is distracting to watch on playback. You should therefore try to minimize this by filming at a set distance for twenty strokes and then zooming in for the close-up shots, if required.

Whilst on the subject of zoom lenses, there is a greater chance of camera shake when you use the lens on its maximum extension, *ie* on maximum zoom (close-up). To minimize this, you should try to have the launch as close to the crew as possible for the particular shot you are filming.

Watching the Video

Now that you have a perfect film of the crew rowing, you can analyse the technique. For

131

maximum effect this needs to be done immediately after the filming session and preferably in between outings, for instance at the weekend, when you have two training sessions. If it is not possible to go back on the water immediately following playback, you should try to spend even five minutes going over the main points just before your next training session.

To optimize the opportunity for learning, it is preferable to watch the entire video, in real time, before making any comments. Each rower should be encouraged to focus on and identify what he is doing well, and only then should he try to identify areas for improvement. As already discussed, rowers should avoid using the word 'faults': they are *not* faults, but opportunities for improving their rowing.

The coach should only offer his views on the video once the crew has gone through it. He should also ask questions to check their understanding of what is required. Simply telling crew members what they are doing 'wrong' or what they need to work on, is no guarantee that they understand how to make the change required. **Without understanding and acceptance of the need to change, no progress will be made.**

Encouraging rowers to analyse other crew members' technique is a policy that can be invaluable in helping to create crew cohesion: if all members offer advice to each other, it is a golden opportunity for the coach to check their level of understanding. I use this technique regularly, and have found it invaluable in dealing with athletes who are not progressing as quickly as I feel they are capable of. If a crew member seems unable to change his technique in the way you have suggested, it may be that he simply does not understand, or accept, what it is you are asking him to do. Asking rowers to analyse other crew members' technique is a good way of identifying where the problem lies.

Depending on what your plan was at the start of filming, there will be many areas that could be looked at during playback. One thing that should *not* be done, however, is to try and assess how many areas you can find that need to be improved. It is far better to confine your observations to the particular technical area you have been working on in the boat. If, for example, you have been trying to improve the timing of the placement of the blades at the catch, you should comment on that, and *not* on whether the boat was balanced or not. As with all learning, progress will come more quickly if you concentrate on one or two areas at most. I then try to find one individual area that each rower has improved upon, and a crew point that has improved as well.

Using Freeze Frame and Slow Motion

Using the slow motion and freeze frame facility offers an ideal opportunity to look at individual differences between the crew. Depending on how proficient its members are, it may be difficult to identify very small differences in timing. As discussed previously, one of the keys to moving a boat efficiently is the timing of the transfer of weight from backstops onto the slide. Using the slow motion facility is one of the best ways of checking for this.

When it comes to both the speed and timing of the catches, the freeze frame button is perfect. By stopping the film when the crew has stopped travelling forwards, and then advancing it frame by frame, it should be possible to assess how long it takes each person to cover the blades at the catch. Counting the number of frames it takes provides an objective measurement of how fast the placement is. This information can then be used to set targets for improvement in the coming weeks.

Freeze frame and slow motion filming of a very fast boat such as an octuple scull can help pinpoint individual areas for improvement.

133

Another area where slow motion and freeze frame are invaluable, is in assessing the work-to-recovery ratio. As with measuring the time taken to cover the blades, it should be possible to freeze the film at the end of the stroke and then advance it, counting the number of frames it takes to reach frontstops. This process can then be repeated as the blades comes through the water to give the ratio between work and recovery. I have found this a very useful exercise when dealing with less experienced rowers for demonstrating to them what the correct ratio should be. You can show them a more accomplished crew and ask them to measure the ratio.

Another way of using this technique, is to measure the differences in ratio for different ratings and boat speeds. This can reinforce the need to have a large ratio at low ratings to achieve the correct ratio at racing speed.

9 Competition Strategies

In order to compete successfully you need to ensure that you are well prepared: there is little point in entering a race and expecting to win if you have not done any training beforehand, for example. There are three main areas you need to consider when preparing for competition: training, which we have already looked at in detail, pre-competition strategies and race strategies.

PRE-COMPETITION STRATEGIES

One of the most often overlooked areas of race preparation is that of the pre-competition strategy (PCS). Opinions differ as to its importance; some coaches and athletes do not take the time to devise an effective PCS, arguing that by the time they get to the competition it is too late to change anything,

Racing at Henley Royal Regatta. (M. Bircumshaw.)

and many others genuinely believe that at this stage it is too late to influence the outcome of the race anyway – after all, if you have not done the right amount, type and quality of training beforehand, you will have little chance of winning. Although this is largely true, failing to devise a properly constructed PCS will in itself reduce the chances of performing to your best. It is for this reason that I believe the time taken to construct a PCS is time well spent.

So what is a PCS, and what is its purpose? It is a plan of action designed to minimize the likelihood of anxiety affecting your performance. The period it covers can vary, but it should be from the end of the previous training session until the end of the competition: this may be anything from one hour in the case of a domestic regatta, to a week for international competitions (or Henley Royal Regatta). The list of areas that need to be considered for possible inclusion in a PCS is potentially endless, and may concern almost any aspect of life over which you have control – and those you do not – such as transport arrangements, food and water, accommodation and equipment.

At its most simple, a PCS may be designed to ensure that you de-rig your boats, load the trailer, arrive in plenty of time to rig your boat and reach the start of the race *on time*. Most of this is common sense of course, but how often do you end up with just one or two people to de-rig the boats and load the trailer? And on race day itself, how often do you see crews turning up late and *rushing* to rig boats and get to the start on time? Is it any wonder that under these circumstances they fail to perform at their best? Having spent the best part of a year preparing for a race, rowing for mile after mile, lifting weights to become stronger, and making countless personal sacrifices, why do crews effectively give their opposition an advantage in this way?

Transport

It makes good sense to ensure that all arrangements regarding transport of equipment and crew to the event are thought out well in advance. And as with all arrangements of this type, it is better to agree with everyone concerned as to who is responsible for doing what. Anything that is left to chance, or is not specifically allocated to someone, will almost certainly not be done. Nor is it any good assuming that everything will be taken care of – it will not. Unless everyone has an agreed task, each person will assume that it is another person's job.

It is also usually a good idea that everyone is agreed as to the best time for de-rigging. This should avoid the problem of only two or three people turning up, or – as is more usual – having some athletes give the excuse immediately after the outing that they have to rush off to a meeting.

It goes without saying that you should allow plenty of time to drive to the regatta: a rule of thumb is to allow an additional hour for every two hours of the estimated travelling time, because it is far better to arrive early and to have to keep yourself occupied for an hour, than to be rushing around to get to the start on time. Similarly, it is better for the crew to arrive at least 2½ hours before the race time, if the boats still need to be rigged; otherwise between 1 and 1½ hours are required.

Finally, when travelling abroad, it is essential to ensure that proper insurance is taken out to cover any breakdown that may occur; the last thing you need is to be stranded in the middle of nowhere with no way of getting to the race.

Accommodation

If you need to stay in a hotel overnight, it is essential that as much information as possible is found out about it before booking. Details should include how far away it is from the regatta, and how long it will take to drive there; how easy it is to get to public transport in case of a breakdown; and perhaps most important, does the hotel have experience in catering for the needs of rowers? Rowers, like most athletes, have their own special requirements, and unless a hotel has a prior experience of dealing with them or has an open-minded approach, problems may very well arise – usually about food.

If you are planning on staying some time, it is a good idea to find out how close the hotel is to the nearest town centre. It makes a big difference if you can walk to the cinema or restaurants, rather than having to spend time in a car or bus.

Crews can become quite isolated if they spend all their time in individual rooms, so ask whether the hotel has communal lounges with a television and video recorder. And does it have a swimming pool, or a gymnasium or similar leisure facility? These may not seem important, but if you are going to be spending more than a day or two at a hotel, you will need to occupy yourself in the hours between practice sessions and racing.

Other details you need to know are, is there a laundry service or easy access to one? If you are spending a week in a hotel, you will accumulate a lot of kit that will need washing (or at least drying), and the situation can be made much worse if the weather is cold and wet. It is not particularly relaxing to be surrounded by heaps of damp, smelly training kit.

It is also worth finding out where the nearest hospital or doctor's surgery is located, particularly when staying abroad.

Food

Rowers have specific nutritional requirements: namely, they need a great deal of food of the right type. If staying at a hotel, check with the head chef that the kitchen will be able to provide the type and quantity of food required. I have been to places where the hotel simply could not understand that we needed about ten times the amount of food that normal people do, and had to pay an additional premium to guarantee that sufficient would be provided. Had I checked beforehand, I could have agreed the price supplement in advance, or gone somewhere else.

Most hotels are willing to help, however, if they have sufficient advance warning of what is required. This allows them to plan their buying and menus, and avoids last-minute problems in the kitchen. It also means they can work out the additional cost involved and decide whether to pass this on to you, and this will help you in preparing the budget for the trip. It is better to know in advance what the likely costs are, than to find out whilst at the regatta that you need to pay more than anticipated.

Where possible I try to agree menus with the hotel in advance so that I know what to expect; it is important to specify what food you would like to be provided. There should be plenty of carbohydrate in the form of pasta, potatoes, rice and bread, as well as meat and vegetables, and the food should not be too greasy.

Water must be available throughout your stay – and this does not mean having to ask the kitchen staff if you can fill up your water bottle. If you are visiting a country where it is doubtful how safe the water is to drink, it is wise to take plentiful supplies with you or to purchase bottled water in bulk when you arrive; the hotel may be happy to store this for you.

If there are vegetarians in the group it is especially useful to agree menus in advance. And a word of warning on this subject: should

It is essential to explain to hotels that vegetarians do not always eat eggs or fish!

some of the group not eat fish or eggs, this must be explained because the term vegetarian can mean different things to different chefs; some will assume that you can eat eggs and fish, others that you eat nothing but salads, and when the chef is in doubt, the old standby of an omelette seems to be the favourite vegetarian dish. This is fine for one meal, but not for every day of the week, as once happened to me! And one final word of advice: very often the vegetarian option will be a pasta dish, which is quite acceptable – but beware of non-vegetarians arriving at the counter first! If they don't like the other food options they won't hesitate to help themselves, which means that by the time the vegetarians arrive, there is no pasta left – the perfect opportunity for the chef to prepare an omelette!

It can be worth asking for breakfast packs to be made up for the lightweight rowers in the group on race days. Those who have travelled with lightweights will be familiar with the scene at the hotel breakfast: as the heavyweight rowers consume as much food as they can, the lightweights surreptitiously stuff as many bread rolls and packs of jam/honey down their shorts as possible, to be eaten at the race-course after the official weigh-in. Far easier to inform the hotel of your requirements – less fun, certainly, but more practical.

Equipment

When travelling to any regatta, common sense dictates that you take as much spare equipment with you as you can. It may not be possible to take a spare boat, but you should certainly take plenty of spare parts, especially those that may be difficult to obtain from other sources. This may seem rather obvious, but it is amazing how often it is overlooked – how often are spare parts assembled the night before the trailer leaves for the regatta, only to find that certain pieces are needed but are not available at such short notice. Had the collection of parts been included in the PCS these could have been ordered in advance.

At the start of the racing season, it is a good idea to designate a regatta box and fill it with all those spare parts that might be needed; it should contain a list detailing the quantities and types of parts contained within, and this list should be kept up to date and new parts ordered as required – there is little point in having a spare parts box which gets progressively emptier as the racing season progresses. It is Murphy's law that the part you need before the final at Henley will be the part that is missing from the box.

RACE STRATEGIES

What should your aims be during the course of the race itself? There are many opinions on the best way to win a race. Some coaches advocate 'blasting off' at the start and then 'hanging on' for the remainder of the race; others favour a more cautious approach, emphasizing the need to maintain an even pace. Whatever your views, just remember there are many ways to win a race, but what matters is that you know the best way for *your* crew to win a *particular* race. It is therefore important to know the strengths and weaknesses of the crew, for without this, you cannot begin to decide what the optimum race strategy might be.

Assessing Your Strengths and Weaknesses

There are three main areas that should be considered when assessing relative strengths and weaknesses: as a rower you should ask yourself how strong you are physiologically, psychologically and technically. One of your physiological strengths may be that you are very fit aerobically and so can maintain a high cruising speed throughout the race. On the other hand you may not have a large anaerobic capacity, which would affect your ability to do bursts of higher speed.

Psychologically you might be very strong, with the ability to row most of the race behind the other crews, confident in the knowledge that you will come through to win in the closing stages. However the reverse could also be true, and perhaps you are liable to panic when your competitors take the lead. You will almost certainly have nerves of some sort on race day, but how will you cope with them?

On the technical side you may be very weak into a head wind, but strong when rowing with a tail wind, or vice versa. Perhaps you can only maintain good technique at a relatively low rating, or maybe it deteriorates rapidly as you become fatigued.

The answers to these questions will provide you with information for your race strategy, and they will also highlight which areas you need to strengthen in your day-to-day training.

Knowing Your Performance Capabilities

Identifying your strengths and weaknesses is only one aspect that needs to be considered when drawing up a race strategy. Another very important factor is your actual performance capability – there would be little point in devising a race strategy that you are simply not capable of doing.

Where possible you should try to assess the following three areas: your **maximum boat speed** (meaning flat-out speed over ten to twenty strokes); **your mean boat speed for the distance you will be racing over**; and the **rating** at which you achieve your mean boat speed. Of these the most important is your mean boat speed: this is normally called your 'cruising' pace and is a vital part of any race strategy.

Cruising Pace

All your training is geared – or should be – towards increasing your cruising pace: this represents the maximum speed you can row at, without accumulating too much lactic acid in your bloodstream. If you do not know what your cruising pace is, how will you know the most efficient speed to row at during the race? Get your pace wrong and you will either 'blow up' before the end of the race, or find yourself feeling too 'fresh' as you approach the line, either of which could cost you a medal.

Identifying your optimum cruising pace has become considerably easier in recent years with the development of the various instruments that measure boat speed; the only way to do this before was to row over a set distance and time how long it took. This was fine as long as you had access to a calm, still stretch of water of the required distance, but with only two 2,000m courses in Great Britain, neither of which can guarantee still conditions, it was difficult to assess cruising pace accurately.

Even with the speed-measuring devices that are available, however, there is still a place for doing regular pieces over a set distance, because there is really no substitute for rowing over the race distance on a regular basis in order to monitor your progress. **Knowing the rate at which you can best achieve your cruising pace is every bit as important as knowing the actual pace itself.** Moreover, for those crews who do not have access to a speed-measuring device, the rating can provide a good indicator of whether or not they are rowing at cruising pace. That said, it is important to remember that the rating is just a number – it is not an infallible guide to boat speed.

Very often it is possible to achieve the same boat speed (or even a higher speed) by dropping the rating a pip or two. One of the interesting side effects of using a speed-measuring device is to see the effect of so-called 'pushes' during a race. I have monitored many crews in this way and can report that in several cases the boat speed actually **dropped** when the crew put in what they thought was their big push!

General Race Tactics

From a physiological point of view, **the most economical way to cover any race distance is to maintain an even pace from start to finish**: this is what the majority of top class, international crews try to do when racing. The problem is that in the real world of racing it is very difficult to achieve.

If we take the example of a 2,000m race, what normally happens is that the first and last 500m are rowed faster than the second and third 500m, and not surprisingly, the first 500m is usually the fastest. Nevertheless, you should still *aim* to row each 500m in the same time, and it may also help to think about rowing both halves of the race in the same time – and if you are to do this, you will need to work hard to maintain your boat speed during the second half of the race. By the time you reach the 1,000m stage, fatigue will have begun to affect your performance, and so it

After 500m there is little to choose between these crews, but which has the fastest cruising speed?

will be essential to focus on maintaining your race pace and race rhythm.

Unfortunately it is at this stage that many crews decide to put in an almighty push to try to break away from the other crews. The trouble is that, rather than consolidating the race pace and rhythm, they strive to increase the rate, but don't actually achieve an increase in boat speed: rather than going faster – or at least maintaining speed – the boat actually slows down! Although it is common practice to try to increase the boat speed during the third 500m, you need to ask yourself why you want to do it, and then what the best way is of achieving it.

The reason for trying to increase the speed at this point in the race is simply to place your-self in a better position to win. Although with good pacing you should not need to do this, there can nevertheless be a strong psycholog-ical advantage in doing so because if you suddenly start to move away from your competitors, they can become unsettled, and may begin to question *their* ability to win. Several studies have shown that anywhere between two-thirds and three-quarters of the way through a race, athletes will ask them-selves two questions: why am I here (this is painful), and can I win; and the answers they come up with will almost certainly influence its outcome. But if you have trained hard, and know you are fit enough to increase your boat speed and then do it, you have a better chance of answering the questions correctly.

141

With regard to the best way of increasing the speed, there are several things to consider: the physiological impact of increasing the speed; the relationship between boat speed and power; and the boat type. As outlined earlier, your cruising pace should represent the maximum speed you can row at without accumulating excessive amounts of lactic acid in your bloodstream. From this it is clear that increasing your boat speed will increase the amount of lactic acid your body produces; and as lactic acid has a negative effect on your ability to produce power, there is a fine line to negotiate between generating more boat speed and producing so much lactic acid that it affects your performance.

Boat Speed versus Power

The other consideration is the disproportionate relationship between boat speed and power: put simply, the faster the boat travels, the greater the resistance created, and the more resistance there is, the greater the amount of power you will need to produce in order to overcome it. In short, you have a two-fold problem because, firstly you need more power just to increase the boat speed, and secondly you need extra power to overcome the greater resistance.

Attempting to increase the boat speed by any significant amount will therefore require a large increase in power which you may or may not be able to sustain until the end of the race. It is also important to realize that varying the boat speed by alternating between cruising pace and short bursts of higher intensity work will actually lead to a *slower* overall time, than rowing at **an even pace for the duration of the race** – provided, of course, that you have rowed at the correct cruising speed.

If, having taken into consideration all the above factors, you still want to increase your boat speed, there are some simple guidelines that will help you achieve it effectively. Basically there are two ways to move your boat more quickly: increase power output per stroke (meaning that the boat travels further per stroke); or increase the rating whilst maintaining power output. If, for example, you are travelling at your optimum cruising speed and rating thirty-six strokes per minute (spm), you can either accelerate the boat past the blade more quickly by applying more power, or take your rate up to 37–38 spm – although as discussed earlier, you should avoid increasing your rating unless you can maintain your power output per stroke.

If you are already travelling at a relatively high speed, it can be very difficult to increase your boat speed by increasing power output alone; this is particularly true for the faster boats such as quadruple sculls and eights. What normally happens in practice, therefore, is that both power output and rating increase – but how do you achieve this? I have experimented with many different ways of increasing the boat speed, with varying degrees of success. What I have found is that if you follow two simple steps, you should be able to achieve the increase in speed you are looking for with the minimum of fuss (and energy).

For most boats you need to focus on increasing power output first by **emphasizing the finish of each stroke**: you should aim to increase the acceleration of the blade through the water – or more properly, the boat past the blade – and then increase the emphasis on applying power at the catch. My crews do two strokes 'sitting back', emphasizing the outside shoulder/arm sequence, followed by two strokes focusing on quickening the hands at the catch (to cover the blade) and 'squeezing off the toes'. If you follow this sequence you can quite easily increase your boat speed, whilst increasing the rating by two pips also. I use this technique to achieve the rating changes required during different training methods, too. In summary, then, you need to do **two strokes working on the finish followed by two strokes working on the catch**.

One thing I cannot emphasize enough is that in crew boats, **any changes made must be done at the same time by all crew members**. It can very tempting, particularly for the stroke person, to try to take the rating up, or to increase the boat speed on his own, but this is incredibly wasteful of energy and ineffective – and yet I see it almost every day of the week.

Who Calls the Shots?

Rowing is all about teamwork, about ensuring that everyone in the crew is able to give 100 per cent of their energy to moving the boat efficiently. If you become frustrated with the balance, for instance, there is little point in banging your hands down at the finish in disgust because this will not make the *boat* balance: what it will do is use up even more of your energy, annoy the rest of the crew and ultimately slow the boat down.

There are few things more annoying than a constant stream of calls from different members of the crew during a race. It is best, therefore, that just one person in the crew calls any changes required. Every crew should decide for itself as to the person best qualified to take on this responsibility, and it is important that the rest of the crew respects him and has the confidence to let him get on with it. Clearly it is better to have someone who is experienced in racing. Many crews choose the bow person simply because of his position in

The 1997 Oxford and Cambridge Boat Race crews passing Chiswick . . .

143

. . . followed by their supporters!

the boat, and this is fine as long as that person is the best for the job; but you may be better off having the rower at three make the calls if he has the greater experience.

Head-of-the-River Races

Although the example used earlier was for a 2,000m race, the same general principles apply to all races, and one of the biggest mistakes that crews make when it comes to head races is to approach them as long training pieces. Time and again I have listened to crews telling me that they found themselves at the halfway stage of the race and realized that they would need to row harder for the second half. As with any race, you need to know what your optimum cruising pace is; there is no point in

waiting until halfway through the race to decide that you can go faster, or that you need to slow down.

One of the keys to head racing (as with other races) is to focus on maintaining your boat speed, and to try to minimize variations in speed. Above all, remember that the hard part of any race is getting the boat up to speed, and from there you should aim to **not let the boat slow down for the rest of the race.**.

Just as with 2,000m racing, you should start off hard for the first two to three minutes, and then settle down into your race pace and race rhythm for the bulk of the course. To finish off, gradually increase your speed as you reach the closing stages of the race.

The other common mistake made in head races is to go off too hard so that you blow up before the halfway point. Once again, the only way to avoid this is to know the crew's capabilities, and to stay within them.

Sprint Races

Sprint races demand the same approach as longer distance races. It is commonly believed that to win sprint races of 500m, for example, you should blast off at the start and hang on for the rest of the course. This is simply not true, however. Even in athletics races, such as the 100m sprint, athletes train for cruising pace; although obviously they also need to develop the ability to accelerate very quickly, there is a substantial part of the race where they are cruising. The only difference between sprint and longer distance races being that the cruising pace will be higher. This means that you need to know **your cruising pace for the length of races that you wish to enter**.

Racing Starts

There are *countless* possible permutations of racing starts and the number, length and power of strokes contained in each can be varied endlessly – but to what end? A racing start serves one purpose only: to transfer the boat from a stationary position to race pace as quickly and efficiently as possible. There is no other reason for doing a racing start, so why do coaches (and rowers) devise so many

The start at Henley Royal Regatta.

combinations to achieve something that is relatively simple?

Watch any top class crew racing and you will see that they all demonstrate the same characteristics off the start: on the first stroke, the boat begins to move forwards gently – it doesn't leap forwards or suddenly begin to accelerate; then during the next five to ten strokes, it gradually increases in speed until the crew has reached the desired speed. This speed is then maintained for anywhere between 200 and 300m, before the crew strides down to its cruising pace.

So, how should you do a racing start? Firstly, **keep it simple**; there is no need for complicated combinations of stroke length. I have heard of so many different combinations, my particular favourite being two three-quarter length, two half-length, one full, a further three-quarter, three full, and finishing off by hitting it for ten. I ask you, do you think *you* could remember all that at the start of a race?

The first stroke should always be the same: you should just **squeeze off the foot stretcher, persuading the boat to move forwards**. If you try to apply too much power on this stroke, you will in fact push the boat backwards. It helps to think about keeping everything parallel/horizontal.

It is particularly important to **minimize any vertical movements** at the start of a race, and to do this it is essential that **the blades are fully covered**, and that any slack is taken up between the swivel and the oar: the oar should be pressed against the face of the swivel.

Somewhere between half- and three-quarter slide is probably about right. It is worth stressing at this stage, that everyone must take the same length of stroke, although this does not necessarily mean that every crew member will have the same body position. All rowers have different lengths of body parts – arms, legs, body – and these differences need to be taken into account when setting up your crew for the racing start (as they do when rigging the boat). For instance, telling everyone to use three-quarter slide will not guarantee that they will take the same length of stroke; and the other thing to remember is that even if you *do* ask everyone to sit at three-quarter slide, they may have different perceptions as to what this is!

The second stroke in a start is normally a bit shorter in length than the first and is generally taken very quickly, but again with the emphasis on pushing off the foot stretcher, rather than lifting the shoulders.

The strokes that follow should quicken gradually in line with the speed of the boat. Never forget that no matter what you do, the boat can only accelerate at a given rate. Thus, during the first few strokes you need to overcome the inertia of the boat, and there is no quick way to do this; it will take time, and nothing you can do will speed it up. In essence what you need to do is develop a feeling for how quickly the boat picks up speed, and adjust your movements accordingly.

Once the boat is moving you need to lengthen out, reaching full slide as economically as possible. Once again, though, this needs to be staged, because you cannot expect to go from half slide to full within two strokes; in practice it may take three or four strokes to reach full slide.

Having reached full slide, the emphasis changes from merely getting the boat moving, to making it move quickly, and this means using maximum power and rating – anything between ten and twenty strokes may be used for this part of the racing start. Talking of the rating, you should not use excessively high rates unless you are capable of applying maximum power at them: **what**

When racing is this close, ensuring a smooth transition to your cruising pace is vital.

matters is how far the boat moves per stroke.

Transition to Cruising Pace

By this time you should be well into the race and so will need to start focusing on other areas, perhaps the most crucial of these being the transition to cruising pace. To my mind, this is one of the most important times in a race. If you do not achieve a smooth transition to your cruising pace, you run the risk of going over the first half of the course at too high a speed, one which you cannot sustain during the second half. But how often do we practise this transition, other than in the race itself?

It is essential to incorporate this transition stage into your weekly training; you simply cannot leave it to chance that you will be able to do it on the day. I make a habit of always incorporating some longer pieces when practising starts, so that the crew can develop the ability to change to cruising pace. The best way of achieving a smooth transition, is simply to hold the legs down a fraction longer at the end of a particular stroke, allowing the rate to come down slightly. This process may be repeated over several strokes if necessary. It should go without saying that **all crew members need to do this at the same time!**

Preparing for Racing

How can you best prepare for your race? First, you should try to incorporate into your

147

training situations that you may face during the race, such as having to row from behind. If you achieve an even pace over the race but end up trailing the other crews, you need to have confidence to know that you will come through them before the finish line. How will you achieve this without having experienced it?

By training alongside another crew it is possible to replicate all manner of race scenarios. For instance, the distance between crews can be staggered at the start of a piece so that the faster crew starts off behind the slower one; in this way it will be having to row from behind, whilst the other will be having to work that bit harder to stay in front. This will benefit both crews, because the slower one will gain the experience of maintaining its technique whilst being pressured by a crew from behind. By alternating the crews throughout the session you can cover a multitude of race situations.

It is also important not to underestimate the effect on a crew of suddenly finding themselves in front of the rest of the field by a considerable distance. This happened in a most spectacular way with one of my crews recently. Having been dumped off the start in the heat, we decided that in the final we needed to start really well. So I geared the crew up for this, emphasizing how vital it was to get off quickly – and the result was that they found themselves in the lead by a considerable margin at the 500m stage, and were still in front at 1,000m; in the final 500m, however, they watched all the crews come back on them, and eventually finished last! Talking with the crew afterwards, they said that it had come as such a shock to them to be in front by so much, that they didn't know what to do and so never really settled into the race.

It is also important to practise each and every stroke of the racing start. Each stroke has a different purpose, and you should focus on this when practising your starts. Thus, if your first stroke could be better, don't practise *ten* stroke starts because you will only mask the inefficiency of the first stroke. What you *should* do, is practise the first stroke until you get it right. You can then focus on the second stroke, and so on until the start is complete. It is also a good idea to practise starts when you are physically and mentally fresh.

Finally, it is important to practise your race tactics during training. You should also agree the tactics you are going to employ during the race several days beforehand; this gives time for everyone to become accustomed to them. On the day of the race itself, all you should need to do is run through them briefly before taking to the water.

After the race you should have a brief meeting, but do not attempt to analyse what happened too thoroughly. Depending on the outcome, it is usually wiser to wait until you can reflect on the race calmly; then you will be able to assess it more rationally and decide where you could have done better, or what tactics worked best.

FINAL THOUGHTS

I hope that you have enjoyed reading this book and that you will be able to use some of the ideas in it to improve your rowing. Before I finish I would like to leave you with one last thought: One of the world's top athletes was once asked the question, 'What is the secret to achieving success?' He replied:

There are three steps to achieving success:
1. Decide what it is you want to achieve;
2. Work out the cost of achieving it;
3. *Pay the price.*

I would add my own thoughts to this: many athletes make it to step 1; some will reach step 2; but **only champions reach step 3**.

I hope that many of you will go on to pay the price.

APPENDIX 1
RECOMMENDED RIGGING MEASUREMENTS FOR CLUB LEVEL CREWS (cm)

BOAT TYPE	MALE (J18 AND ABOVE)				FEMALE (J18 AND ABOVE)			
	SPREAD (TD)	LENGTH OF OARS (MACON)	LENGTH OF OARS (CLEAVER)	INBOARD	SPREAD (TD)	LENGTH OF OAR (MACON)	LENGTH OF OAR (CLEAVER)	INBOARD
2–	86	382	374	116	86	378	371	116
2+	87	382	374	117	–	–	–	–
4–	85	382	374	115	85	378	371	115
4+	85.5	382	374	115.5	85.5	378	371	115.5
8+	84	382	374	114	84	378	371	114
1X	159	298	288	88	159	296	286	88
2X	158	298	288	87.5	158	296	286	87.5
4X	158	300	291	87.5	158	298	288	87.5

BOAT TYPE	MALE (J16)				FEMALE (J16)			
	SPREAD (TD)	LENGTH OF OARS (MACON)	LENGTH OF OARS (CLEAVER)	INBOARD	SPREAD (TD)	LENGTH OF OAR (MACON)	LENGTH OF OAR (CLEAVER)	INBOARD
2–	86	380	–	116	86	376	–	116
4–	85	380	–	115	85	376	–	115
4+	85.5	380	–	115.5	85.5	376	–	115.5
8+	84	380	–	114	84	376	–	114
1X	159	296	–	87.5	159	294	–	87.5
2X	158	296	–	87	158	294	–	87
4X	158	298	–	87	158	296	–	87

PLEASE NOTE

The essential difference in the recommended rig between male and female rowers is the *length* of oar. This is also true of junior 16 rowers. The above recommendations are designed to provide a starting point for experimentation. Do not attempt to use these rigs with oars that are longer than those stated as this will significantly increase the work load. If you do not have oars of the correct length of oar you may need to ease the load by increasing (a) the inboard or (b) the span. For younger rowers the oars should ideally be shorter still. For more information see Chapter 4.

Appendix 2
ARA Sample Water Training Sessions
Preparation Period (Oct–March)

Type	Reps/Sets	Rate	%Max Heart Rate	Heart Rate (bpm)	Rest
UT2	1×30–45'	18–22	65–75%	130–150	None
UT2	1×60–120'	18–22	65–75%	130–150	None
UT1	1×45–60'	20–24	75–85%	150–170	None
UT1	2–3×20' 5' each rating	16–18–20–22 18–20–22–24 16–18–20–22	75–85%	150–170	None
UT1	4–6×10' (4'+3'+2'+1')	18–20–22–24	70–85%	150–170	None
AT	1×30–40'	24–26	85–90%	170–180	None
AT	2–3×20'	24–28	85–90%	170–180	8–10'
AT	20'+20'+20'	24+26+28	85–90%	170–180	None
AT	2–3×12'	26–28	85–90%	170–180	8–10'
AT	2–4×10'	26–28	85–90%	170–180	8–10'
TR	2–3×10' (4'+3'+2'+1')	24+26+28+30	80–95%	160–190	8–10'
TR	2–3×10' (4'+3'+2'+1')	26+28+30+32	85–95%	170–190	8–10'
TR	2–3×7' (3'+2'+1'+1')	28+30+32+34	85–95%	170–190	8–10'
TR	2–3×2000m (6–9')	26–28	90%	175–185	8–10'
TR	3–8×5'	26–28	90–95%	180–190	6–8'
TR	6–10×3'	28–30	90–95%	180–190	5'
LT	None				
A–LT	None				

Competition Period (April–Aug)

Type	Reps/Sets	Rate	%Max Heart Rate	Heart Rate (bpm)	Rest
UT2	1×30–45'	18–22	65–75%	130–150	None
UT2	1×60–120'	18–22	65–75%	130–150	None
UT1	1×60–90'	20+24	65–80%	130–160	None
	alternate 5' rating 20 and 24				
UT1+A–LT	1×60' +10–15 stroke bursts (A–LT)	18 rating 32–34 every 5'	65–95%	130–180	None
UT1	1×60–90'	22–26	75–85%	150–170	None
UT1	2–3×20' 5' each rating	18–20–22–24 20–22–24–26 18–20–22–24	75–85%	150–170	5'
AT	2–3×30'	25+27+29	85–90%	170–180	None
AT	2–3×12'	28–30	85–90%	170–180	8–10'
AT	2–4×10'	28–30	85–90%	170–180	8–10'
TR	2–3×10' (4'+3'+2'+1')	26–28–30–32 or 28–30–32–34	80–95%	160–190	8–10'
TR	2–4×7' (3'+2'+1'+1')	30–32–34–36	85–95%	170–190	8–10'
TR	2×2000m	30–34	90–95%	180–190	10–15'
TR	2–3×1500m	28–30–32 30–32–34 28–30–32	90–95%	180–190	10–12'
TR	3–6×5'	28–32	90–95%	180–190	8–10'
TR	4–8×3'	32–34	90–95%	180–190	6–8'
TR	2–3×(10×20/(10/L))	30–36	90–95%	180–190	8–10'
TR	1–2×(10×30/(15/L))	32–36	90–95%	180–190	8–10'
TR	1–2×(10×17/(5/L))	32–34	90–95%	180–190	8–10'

COMPETITION PERIOD (APRIL–AUG) PRE-COMPETITION WEEK AND PREVIOUS WEEKEND ONLY

Type	Reps/Sets	Rate	%Max Heart Rate	Heart Rate (bpm)	Rest
UT2	1×60–90'	18–20	65–75%	130–150	None
TR	2×1500m	32–34	90–95%	180–190	8–10'
TR	2×(5–10×30/(10/L))	32–36	90–95%	180–190	8–10'
LT	3–6×500m	Max	Max	Max	2–3'
LT	2–4×1000m	Max	Max	Max	5–10'
LT	1×1000m				
	1×500m	Max	Max	Max	10'
	1×250m				
A–L	1×30', with 6–12×10–15/max rating bursts	18–20	65–95%	150–190	None

NOTE:

1. These models assume an AT of 170–180.
2. Rate for a Single should be two less per minute.
3. Codes used are as follows: ' = minutes, " = seconds and / = strokes

154

Index